THE OLD FARMER'S ALMANAC

Book of Weather Lore

THE OLD FARMER'S ALMANAC

Book of Weather Lore

The fact and fancy behind weather predictions, superstitions, old-time sayings, and traditions.

By Edward F. Dolan

Foreword by Willard Scott

YANKEE® BOOKS

A division of Yankee Publishing Incorporated
Dublin, New Hampshire

To Rose

Edited by Sandra Taylor
Designed by Jill Shaffer
Illustrated by Carl Kirkpatrick

Yankee Publishing Incorporated
Dublin, New Hampshire 03444

First Edition

Library of Congress Cataloging-in-Publication Data

Dolan, Edward F., 1924-
The old farmer's almanac book of weather lore: the fact and fancy behind weather predictions, superstitions, old-time sayings, and traditions. / by Edward Dolan; foreword by Willard Scott. — 1st ed.
p. cm.
Bibliography: p.
Includes index.
ISBN 0-89909-165-2 : $15.95
1. Weather — Folklore. I.Title. II. Title: Book of weather lore.
QC998.D65 1988 88-14018
551.6'31 — dc 19 CIP

Contents

Foreword

I HAVE A NEIGHBOR in Virginia who is ninety-five. His name is Eddie Strother. One of my favorite memories of Eddie will always be his 90th birthday party.

Eddie is a farmer . . . a real farmer who works and manages a 400-acre farm in northern Virginia and who also works in the local bank. When I asked Eddie when he planned to retire, he looked at me and sucked on his pipe and answered, "When I retire to what? . . . Let me tell you something, Scottie, I'd rather *work* out than *rust* out." I think there are volumes of truth in these statements.

So you don't see what this has to do with *The Old Farmer's Almanac Book of Weather Lore?* Well, most weather lore comes from old farmers, and most old farmers have a pretty good philosophy when it comes to living. In fact, one of the first pieces of weather lore I ever heard about came from Eddie Strother.

Down in our part of Virginia, one weather tradition we follow is to wait until after the dogwood blossoms turn brown before we plant our corn. It has been my experience over the past thirty years of gardening that, by the time the blossoms have turned brown, the last killing frost has occurred and that is indeed the time to plant corn to be sure it will be free from frost.

Let us always remember that the first weathermen (pardon me, weather *persons* — let's not forget the ladies) were farmers. Farmers and fishermen depended on the weather for their livelihood, not to mention their personal safety.

Two of our most prominent founding fathers were students of the weather: Thomas Jefferson, himself a farmer, was the official weatherman for the First Congress of the United States during the hot summer days in 1776, when our Constitution was being written in Philadelphia. And Benjamin Franklin, after two quarts of brandy (and maybe being not too safety-minded), flew a kite during an electrical storm and discovered the principle of electricity. . . a weather-related fact.

The National Weather Service in the United States is just a little over one hundred years old, so official weather records have been kept only for the past century or so. Prior to that, all weather information was provided by almanacs and personal diaries of seafaring men and especially farmers. There is no question that, before satellites and weather recording devices were available, farmers got their information by observing nature year after year and by correlating the times they planted their crops with the weather conditions that existed at those times. So much of what is known as weather lore is, indeed, weather fact.

A favorite bit of weather lore passed along to me was that if you are bitten by a turtle, he will not let go until there is a clap of thunder. I have not personally experienced this, but I would choose to think this is an old superstition. I can, however, vouch for certain native signs concerning weather. When large flocks of birds fly wildly about in the fall or when there is great activity among spiders around a door jamb in your home in the fall, there will, without a doubt, be a dramatic drop in temperature. Smoke going down rather than rising up a chimney, certain sounds of wood burning in a fire (both of which happen to be my father's favorite ways of predicting snow) may or may not be as accurate as the National Weather Service forecasting a 40% chance of precipitation, but the romance, the fun, and the mystery involved all add up to that great mystical science we call weather forecasting.

Any sincere, honest student of the weather will tell you that weather forecasting, even with today's increasingly sophisticated instruments, including satellites, is no more than a guessing science. While the accuracy of predicting weather has improved somewhat over the past one hundred years, it is still far from perfect, and (in my opinion and in the opinion of those who know far more about the subject than I do) weather forecasting will never be 100% accurate.

To steal a line from Henny Youngman, the National Weather Service is still twelve hours behind arthritis.

— WILLARD SCOTT
Weather forecaster for
NBC's "Today" show

ACKNOWLEDGMENTS

My thanks to Dr. Richard M. Head and Mr. Robert S. Ingram for reviewing my manuscript and passing along their helpful comments.

INTRODUCTION

An Endangered Species

> *Red sky at night, sailor's delight.*
> *Red sky in the morning, sailor's warning.*

> *When the wind is in the east,*
> *'Tis neither good for man nor beast.*

> *The winds of daytime wrestle and fight*
> *Longer and stronger than those of the night.*

> *It is bad luck to point at a rainbow.*

> *Young girls are to go outside early of a May morning and cleanse their faces with dew. Then they will be beautiful all the year.*

> *The sun is a giant ship in which the Egyptian sun god Ra carries the dead across the azure sea of the sky to their final resting place.*

THESE ARE BUT six of the seemingly countless folk predictions, comments, superstitions, traditions, and beliefs that make up the age-old literature of weather lore. In common with all that has been written into the literature down through the centuries, certain of the six, as we shall see in the coming pages, are grounded in solid truth. Some have a grain of truth to them and can prove themselves valid at times or in certain locales. Some are false. And some are imaginative, but nevertheless mere fancies. But, from the most valid to the most fanciful, they all have one thing in common. They are members of what may be an endangered species. The worldwide literature to which they belong seems to be vanishing rapidly from human use and memory.

Responsible in part for the threatened disappearance is this century's respect (sometimes deserved and sometimes not) for science and the learned expert. The traditions and superstitions, for example, that make up so much of weather lore are greeted with a casual and often amused disdain — while the beliefs, dating back to the most ancient of times, are dismissed out of hand because we have been taught to know better. The weather predictions that abound everywhere in the literature are set aside in favor of today's scientific and highly, though by no means completely, dependable systems of forecasting.

All this is a pity. In our disdain for the superstitions, misguided though some assuredly are, we overlook the energetic, leaping imagination and the untiring quest for an understanding of the mysterious that went into them. When we forget the traditions and beliefs, we forget that they represent a reverence for the unknown and a yearning to interpret and make sense of it. In both instances, we have lost a degree of kinship with all those who have gone before us and a full understanding of that most basic of facts — that we are not alone and separate, the products of an individual and supposedly advanced age, but are the participants in a continuing history.

As for the myriad predictions: little more than a century ago, Ralph Waldo Emerson, in his essay "Self-Reliance," chided civilized man for having a fine "Geneva watch" but forgetting the skill of telling the hour by the sun. Much the same can be said today of our weather forecasting, and of so many of our other endeavors. Our forefathers looked to the sky, the earth, the animal life all around, and even their own overworked joints and muscles for word of what the weather planned next, but we have turned the job over to others — the television forecasters with their crayons and pointers, and the newspaper with its complex charts from the National Weather Service. In the process, we have forgotten how to look for ourselves.

Because so many of our forebears — in particular, those who were seamen and farmers — depended on the weather for their livelihoods and their very lives, observations about the weather were born out of necessity as well as curiosity. Whatever their reasons, and no matter how mistaken their conclusions could be at times, their search made them more at one with the nature around them. Today, our personal observations and forecasting are done simply out of curiosity and for the pleasure of studying our own natural surroundings. Yet, ironically, in a time when concrete and steel are so prevalent that they cause us to lament our separation from all that is natural, we have voluntarily surrendered the joy and education derived from lifting our eyes and gauging for ourselves what the sky is doing or going to do.

If what we have lost already is a pity, then it will be a greater pity to lose the literature itself. It is a treasure house of folklore in which are found all the elements of thinking — everything from magnificent insights at the one extreme to foolish and deluded notions at the other. A look at just a few weather predictions and superstitions proves the point. First, there are the splendid truths, splendid because they are drawn not from the laboratory, the textbook, or the schoolroom but from simple, yet so very shrewd, everyday observations:

> *A cow with its tail to the west*
> *Makes weather the best.*
> *A cow with its tail to the east*
> *Makes weather the least.*

The possible truths:

> *If corn husks are thicker than usual, a cold winter lies ahead.*

The gritty humor (in this instance, New England):

> *Dirty days hath September,*
> *April, June, and November.*
> *From January to May,*
> *The rain it raineth every day.*
> *All the rest have thirty-one,*
> *Without a blessed gleam of sun.*
> *And if any of them had two-and-thirty,*
> *They'd be just as wet and twice as dirty.*

The all-too-human errors:

> *Lightning never strikes twice in the same place.*

The all-too-human fears:

> *If St. Elmo's Fire stays high in the masts, it means good luck and a safe voyage. If it comes down low in the rigging or to the deck, it signals bad luck.*

The odd fancies:

> *The ends of the rainbow stand in a river. Anyone who crawls to the river on hands and knees and then drinks the water from which the rainbow is rising will instantly change sex.*

And charming fancies:

> *If it rains on or about St. Mary Magdalen's Day* [July 22], *she is washing her kerchief to have it clean and ready for the festival held on July 25, the feast day of her cousin, St. James the Great.*

Furthermore, the literature is a truly international one. Though most of the weather lore known in the United States was either born here or came to us from Europe (and is the lore to which this book will principally devote itself), the literature has received contributions from every culture and nation in the world. To mention but a few:

> *The corn is as comfortable under the snow as an old man under his fur cloak.*
>
> — RUSSIA

> *The sun is the celestial ancestor from whom our rulers are descended.*
>
> — JAPAN AND PERU

> *Women must never look at the moon for more than a moment or so. It incites them to orgies.*
>
> — GREENLAND ESKIMOS

> *When the frog croaks in the meadow,*
> *There will be rain in three hours' time.*
>
> — INDIA

On top of all else, it is a literature that has been produced by the most diverse group of contributors ever assembled. In their sharing of a universal interest, they have come together from all walks of life. They range from farmers, shepherds, ranchers, and seamen to backyard meteorologists and some of the most distinguished names in the histories of literature, philosophy, politics, and science. From widely separated eras and locales, here is what just three of the most honored have had to say:

> *If on her cheeks you see the maiden's blush,*
> *The ruddy moon foreshadows that winds will rush.*
>
> — VIRGIL (70–19 B.C.)
> From: *Georgics*

The weary sun hath made a golden set,
And, by the bright track of his fiery car,
Gives signal of a goodly day to-morrow.

— WILLIAM SHAKESPEARE (1564–1616)
From: *King Richard III*

For I fear a hurricane;
Last night the moon had a golden ring,
And tonight no moon we see.

— HENRY W. LONGFELLOW (1807–1882)
From: "Wreck of the Hesperus"

In the coming pages, we will look at this literature of weather lore and at the meteorological forces that render some of it true, some partly true, and some totally false. But a word of caution is in order. Because our subject is weather lore, this book is not intended to be a treatise on the science of the weather. The passages on that science are written with two specific goals in mind: (1) to provide information sufficient for an understanding of why a folk prediction or outlook is valid to one extent or another, or completely wide of the mark; and (2) to provide the scientific material necessary for a basic grasp of how forceful the elements are that have inspired the literature of weather lore.

This being the case, certain topics, the destructive tornado among them, will be mentioned only briefly or not at all because they actually play no role in weather lore; others, such as the rain and the winds, will receive a lion's share of attention because they are responsible for a lion's share of the lore. For those interested in looking more deeply into the science of the weather — its causes and workings — the volumes that were consulted in the preparation of this book should prove both entertaining and informative. They are listed in the section entitled Recommended Reading, which begins on page 218.

One of the most interesting is *Signal Service Notes No. IX: Weather Proverbs,* which was published by the Government Printing Office in 1883. Ordered by and then prepared under the direction of Maj. General W. B. Hazen, Chief Signal Officer of the U.S. Army, the book ranks as a classic collection of American weather lore. The book itself was written by 1st Lieutenant H. H. C. Dunwoody. It is still to be found in many libraries and makes fascinating reading.

CHAPTER ONE

Companion and Dictator: Our Weather

> *Oh, what a blamed uncertain thing*
> *This pesky weather is;*
> *It blew and snew and then it thew,*
> *And now, by jing, it friz.*
>
> — PHILANDER JOHNSON (1866–1939)

IT IS A PRETTY sure bet that, among the topics discussed most often, the weather will rank among the top ten. With its capacity, in Johnson's words, to blew, snew, thew, and friz — not to mention its ability to burn us dry or soak us through to the skin — the weather has been capturing our attention daily for as long as our kind have been on this planet. No one will argue the fact that, at one or more points in the course of any day, we all stop and look at the weather, either to praise or curse it, and most assuredly to talk about it. Such talk, in one form or another, is age-old and all too familiar to all of us. It is talk that has been duly noted through the passing years by some of the world's most distinguished weather watchers:

> *Everybody talks about the weather but nobody does anything about it.*
>
> — Attributed variously to: MARK TWAIN (1835–1910) and CHARLES DUDLEY WARREN (1829–1900)

> *What would have become of us had it pleased Providence to make the weather unchangeable? Think of the destitution of the morning callers.*
>
> — SYDNEY SMITH (1771–1845)
> From: *Lady Holland's Memoir*

> *When two Englishmen meet, their first talk is of the weather.*
>
> — SAMUEL JOHNSON (1709–1784)

It is talk that sired the vast collection of folk wisdom and error known as weather lore. That it did so — and that it has been so widespread — is anything but surprising, for the weather touches all of us. Through the ages it has triggered endless passing comments as well as seemingly immortal axioms.

For each of us, the weather is a daily companion that accompanies us throughout life. It governs — or, at the very least, influences — virtually every aspect of our lives: the types of homes we live in, the clothing we choose for work and leisure, the kinds of vacations we take, the heating and air conditioning bills we pay, and, in many instances, the places where we must go to earn our livings and the seasons in which we are able to work.

But what exactly are we talking about when we speak of this force that, in its dictatorial companionship, generates so much talk and has prompted such a vast body of folklore? What entity do we have in mind? Quite often, in our talk, we confuse it with a close relative, climate. Weather is the term used to describe the momentary or day-by-day behavior of the atmosphere at any spot on the earth, and climate is defined as the general type of weather routinely enjoyed or suffered, year after year, in a given area. It is necessary to differentiate between the two early on because the folklore in this book derives almost exclusively from the various behaviors and moods of the weather — not from the characteristics of the climate.

BEHAVIORS AND MOODS

Those behaviors and moods are, indeed, various and fascinating and, at times, maddening. Topping the list of the weather's abilities to fascinate and trouble is its changeability, a talent that long ago inspired New Englanders to say:

> | *If you don't like the weather, wait a few moments.*

As far as Mark Twain was concerned, the saying ranked as one of nature's great truths. When addressing the New England Society in 1876,* he told his audience that he thought their weather was made by "new apprentices" who were being trained in "the weather-chief's factory" in exchange for their "board and clothes." At his acid best, he commented:

> There is a sumptuous variety about the New England weather that compels the stranger's admiration — and regret. The weather is always doing something there; always attending strictly to business; always getting up new designs and trying them on the people to see how they will go. But it gets through more business in the spring than any other season. In the spring, I have counted one hundred and thirty-six different kinds of weather inside four-and-twenty hours.

Then his fancy took full flight:

> It was I that made the fame and fortune of that man that had that marvelous collection of weather on exhibition at the Centennial, that so astonished the foreigners. He was going to travel all over the world and get specimens from all the climes. I said,

---

* Mark Twain's "Speech on the Weather" was given at the New England Society's 71st annual dinner in New York City, December 22, 1876. (From *The Family Mark Twain.* New York: Harper & Row Publishers, Inc., 1975.)

> "Don't do it; you come to New England on a favorable spring day." I told him what we could do in the way of style, variety, and quantity. Well, he came and he made his collection in four days. As to variety, why he confessed that he got hundreds of kinds of weather that he had never heard of before. And as to quantity — well, after he had picked out and discarded all that was blemished in any way, he not only had weather enough, but weather to spare; weather to hire out; weather to sell; to deposit; weather to invest; weather to give to the poor.

Granted, Twain was letting fly with some broad exaggeration for comic effect. But, at base, he was talking fact. New England weather *is* changeable, ambitiously so, a fact that accounts for the flood of New England proverbs and predictions in this book. But the weather is quite as capricious in other parts of the United States. Midwesterners know only too well that a peaceful summer sky can swiftly turn black or sea-green and produce a torrential rain or a deadly tornado. There's no need to tell Washingtonians or Hawaiians of how abruptly rain can put in an appearance. Californians, especially those living along the northern part of the state's coast, may hate to admit it, but fog, showers, unexpected winds, or, conversely, the absence of anticipated sea breezes regularly contradict the myth that theirs is a weather eternally blissful.

But the weather's changeability is not, of course, restricted to the United States. The people of the Bavarian Alps are more than familiar with the hailstones, sometimes of golf-ball size, that can suddenly fling themselves from the sky in spring and summer. And, when speaking of changeability, we need to mention just one country to drive the point home: Great Britain. There are visitors who will swear that they've seen areas of the British Isles blithely go through four seasons all in a single day.

The weather in any locale is not only capable of changing itself in a matter of minutes or hours, but is just as capable of altering itself from place to place within that locale. San Franciscans, to cite just one case in point, have long had a variation of the earlier-mentioned New England saying: "If you don't like the weather, walk a few blocks." They know what they're talking about. A stroll of a mere two or three blocks can take you out of an area where fog and wind are almost perennial callers and into a neighborhood where sunlight is the usual order of the day.

With a slight alteration from "walk a few blocks" to "drive a few miles," the San Francisco saying can be just as well applied to the entire Bay Area. On a July day, unwary out-of-staters who arrive in San Francisco with only lightweight wear may well shiver in fog with temperatures in the 50°s while 30 miles to the north, the city of San Rafael basks in 70° to 80° sunshine and, little more than an hour's drive eastward, the state capital, Sacramento, swelters in 100° heat.

But its talent for change is only one facet of the weather's personality. It is quite as willing to behave in a routine and predictable fashion — bringing annual monsoons to southern Asia; locking Indonesia and, far away in another hemisphere, the American South and Midwest in long summers of searing, humid heat; cooling and even chilling the furnacelike Sahara and the western U.S. deserts on summer nights; bestowing regions virtually everywhere with the bud-opening warmth of spring; giving Europe and the United States the crisp and multicolored days of autumn, the sometimes sudden but always lazy heat of late year (Indian summer in the United States and St. Luke's summer in Europe), and then the leaden skies of winter.

Every day we live with this multifaceted personality that is so predictable at one extreme and so fickle at the other. When agreeable, it can do anything from permit us to make a living to move us deeply with its artistry as it sculpts a creamlike cloud or turns the horizon into a palette of unforgettable colors. When out of sorts, it can destroy crops; spoil a family outing; startle or frighten us with thunder and lightning; threaten or even take our lives with rainstorms, floods, hurricanes, and tornadoes. In all, it is that ever-present dictatorial companion.

WHY THE DICTATOR?

The answer begins with the vision of our planet tracing its endless, elliptical path through space, spinning on its axis at the approximate rate of one revolution every 24 hours, and circling the sun once every 365 days. Girdling the earth and pressing in on it as it travels are five layers of atmosphere. The outermost of their number is the exosphere, as yet a little understood expanse that begins 500 miles above the earth and may stretch into space to a distance of perhaps 1,000 miles. The innermost is the troposphere, the layer in which we live. It ranges upwards from the earth's surface for between 10 and 12 miles at the equator and averages just under 6 miles thick at the Poles.

In between lie, in ascending order, the stratosphere (extending some 30 miles above the troposphere); the mesosphere (stretching another 50 miles); and the thermosphere, which ascends to the exosphere.

The atmospheric layers consist of a wide variety of gases, some of which are found mainly within certain tiers (an example is the poisonous ozone, which is almost absent near the earth's surface but is at maximum concentration in the lower levels of the stratosphere). The principal gases are nitrogen (accounting for 78% of the atmosphere) and oxygen (about 21%). Such other gases as argon, carbon dioxide, hydrogen, helium, krypton, methane, and nitrous oxide make up the remaining 1%. Additionally, the atmosphere contains water vapor, plus, especially at its lowest levels, dust, smoke, carbon monoxide, sea salt, industrial and domestic smoke, and micro-organisms.

Of the five layers, the troposphere, obviously, is the one that interests us most. In part because of the earth's gravitational pull and in part because the layers press down on one another, the troposphere contains the heaviest concentration of atmosphere.

The troposphere has often been described as an "ocean of air,"

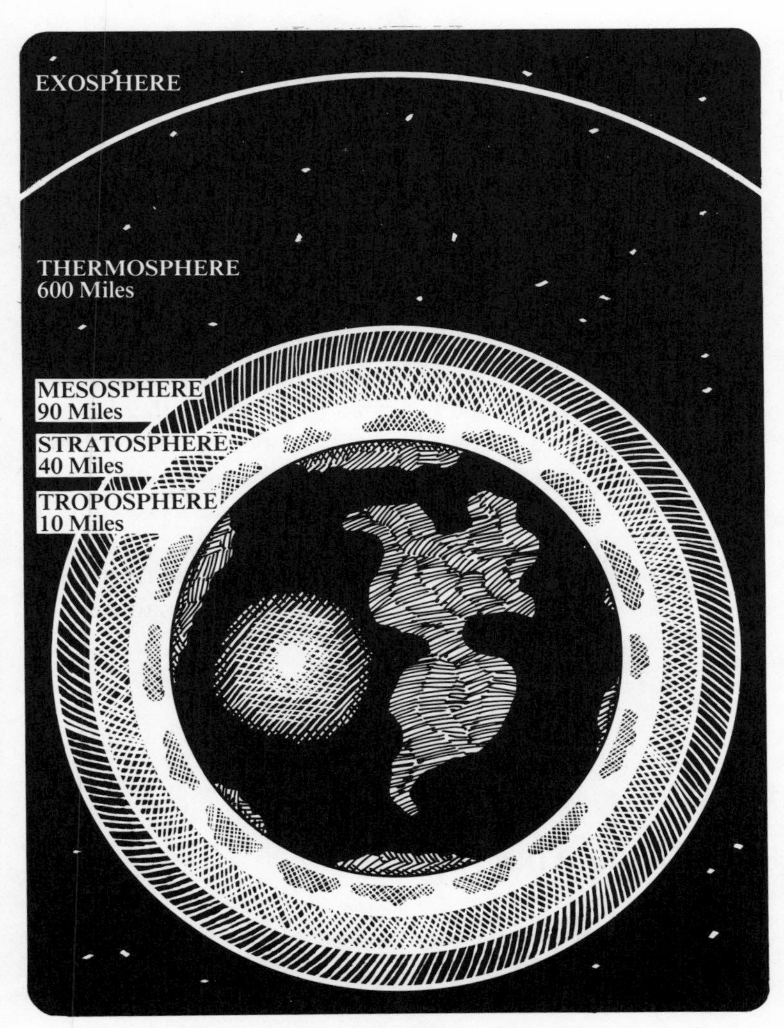

THE FIVE ATMOSPHERIC BANDS *extending outward from the earth's surface are the troposphere, the stratosphere, and the mesosphere. Beyond them are the thermosphere and the exosphere. The troposphere, which contains the heaviest concentration of atmosphere, is where our weather is produced.*

with the earth's surface being its sea bed. The description is an apt one. Just as water pressure is greatest along the floors of the world's oceans, so is air pressure heaviest at the earth's surface. And, as the movement of water disturbs an ocean floor and influences the lives of the creatures living there, so do the various actions of the atmosphere disturb its "sea bed" and influence the lives of the creatures there. Those actions, from the gentlest to the harshest, make up our weather. They are triggered by four elements — moisture, pressure, wind, and the increase and decrease of heat.

Without these elements, we would still have what could be called weather, but it would be unchanging. All weather is born within and confined to the thickly atmosphered troposphere. Where there is no atmosphere, there can be no weather. The moon, for example, is a weatherless planet because it is without a surrounding atmosphere. Were we able to live there, as one day we may, we would be without such bothers as rainstorms and raging winds. But we would also be without that fascinating body of folk wisdom and error known as weather lore.

WEATHER LORE

> *Goodness, how we'd like to know*
> *Why the weather alters so.*

— FORD MADOX FORD (1873–1939)
From: "Children's Song"

Along with our abiding interest in the weather, two other forces within us are responsible for our weather lore — our desire to read the future and our yearning to fathom the mysterious. If there is one thing that we humans have wanted to do ever since we invented the word "future," it is to guess what it holds for us. This is an urge that dates back to the most ancient of times and continues to be as strong in us as it ever was. It prompted our forebears to develop astrology, the tarot deck, and the crystal ball. In one form, it remains with us today in the newspaper's daily horoscope and, in another, in all those university "think tanks" dedicated to gauging what life will be like in the rapidly approaching new century or when, if ever, nuclear warfare breaks out. Playing two of our most basic instincts — fear and hope — against each other, predicting the future cannot help being one of our most basic urges.

The weather takes a back seat to no other topic when we get down to guessing the future. All of us today — from the simply curious to those who might be accommodated or inconvenienced by its moods and on to those whose livelihoods hinge on what the skies plan — have at hand a variety of helpers to facilitate our guesswork. There are the forecasters who have become fixtures on every radio and television station. There are the private meteorologists who supply daily predictions for outdoor industries. There are the National Weather Service's mapped prognostications in the daily newspaper. And there are the nation's many weather centers, all able to warn us instantly of approaching rains, hurricanes, and tornadoes.

But what of the days before the science of meteorology took shape, before modern forecasting and our widespread systems of communication came into being? We turned in several directions for help. First, from the earliest of times, we relied on our eyes and minds. We looked at the behaviors exhibited by the sky, the ground underfoot, the surrounding plants and trees, our animals, and even our own aches and pains. When a behavior occurred several times (or perhaps, on occasion, only once) and was followed by a certain kind of weather, we began to see it as betokening that kind of weather. We put what we saw into comments and proverbs to serve us as guides and to be passed down through the years for the benefit of generations to come. The proverbs often rhymed because versification was a popular mode of expression and an aid to the memory. Thus was born the likes of:

> *If the robin sings in the bush,*
> *Then the weather will be coarse.*
> *If the robin sings on the barn,*
> *Then the weather will be warm.*

And thus was born weather lore.

Second, we did not work alone or simply in the company of our neighbors. Early on, we received help from three outside sources. Though not listed in chronological order, there was, first, the Bible, which contains such weather data as:

> *When it is evening, ye say it will be fair weather: for the sky is red. And in the morning, it will be foul weather today: for the sky is red and lowering.*
>
> — MATTHEW 16: 2,3

Next, there were those writers and scientists of every era who were also devout weather watchers; we saw samples of their work in the Introduction to this book and will encounter more in the coming pages.

And, finally, there was the almanac, which dates back to the Egypt of 3000 B.C. From its very inception, the almanac provided a variety of information of value especially to those whose livelihoods and very lives depended on the whims of the weather — the farmer and seaman. Benjamin Franklin's *Poor Richard's Almanack* for 1733 was following an ancient tradition when, as advertised on its cover, it presented the following assorted wonders:

> . . . The Lunations, Eclipses, Judgment of the Weather, Spring Tides, Planets Motions & mutual Aspects, sun and Moon's

> Rising and Setting, Length of Days, Time of High Water, Farm, Courts, and observable Days.
>
> Fitted to the Latitude of Forty Degrees and a Meridian of Five Hours West from London, but may without Sensible Errors Serve all the Adjacent Places, even from Newfoundland to South Carolina.

In its earliest forms, the almanac was written on papyrus, etched in stone, or printed on wooden planks or blocks. The term itself comes from the Arabic word with the poetic meaning "calendar of the sky." In the several centuries between the invention of the printing press and the founding of the modern weather service, the almanac proved to be one of the publishing industry's best money-makers. Literally thousands of different almanacs poured out of European, Asian, and American print shops. They were eagerly awaited and even more eagerly grabbed up on publication. For the farmer, the seaman, the businessman, and the family, they were the sole source of needed weather information. Much of that information, cranked out by printers and writers who were anything but accomplished meteorologists, was miles wide of the truth. But the information that did prove accurate, even if by sheer coincidence, was greeted with awe and never forgotten. Just one on-the-mark entry could make an almanac's reputation and see it trusted for years to come. Much of what these little books had to say, both the accurate and inaccurate, has become a cherished part of weather lore.

But the literature of weather lore cannot be limited to our desire to read the future. That yearning has always been accompanied by the equally deep — if not even deeper — urge to understand and make sense of all that is mysterious around us. Out of this yearning came the myriad ancient beliefs, superstitions, and rituals that we'll soon be discussing. Most were devised not only to explain and thus better understand the bewildering and often frightening weather and the forces that were — or were thought to be — behind it, but also to achieve a degree of control over its moods through reverential attitudes that would invite its best behavior. Into the literature of weather lore they have all gone to give it some of its most fascinating pages.

* * *

And now it's time to turn to that literature itself to see what it had to say — and still has to say. As was stressed in the Introduction, we're about to encounter much that is true, partly true, or totally false, and much that may strike us as empty and even silly superstition and practice. But all the proverbs and the observations that brought them into being, all the rituals, and all the beliefs share a single trait. Each speaks with eloquence of the vaulting, never idle imagination that is mankind's.

CHAPTER TWO

A Sky of Sun and Sunlight

AT NIGHT, THE stars emerge and lie together in vast clusters and configurations across the vault of the sky. The moon rises to join them. But in the daytime hours, the sun drives all away and reigns by itself, needing no companion as it travels across the heavens. Thus, seen as courageous because of its aloneness, it was to the world's earliest peoples a hero. And, because of its heat and light, it was recognized as a mighty force in the shaping of their lives — perhaps the mightiest of all the natural forces that surrounded and mystified them. In the centuries ever since, homage has been paid to that aloneness and majesty in lines such as:

> *The sun sees all things and discovers all things.*
>
> — CICERO (106–43 B.C.)

> *The Sunne shineth indifferently ouer* [sic] *all.*
>
> — ENGLAND, 16th CENTURY

> *Whence are thy beams, O sun! thy everlasting light? Thou comest forth in thy awful beauty; the stars hide themselves in the sky; the moon, cold and pale, sinks in the western wave. But thou, thyself, movest alone.*

— JAMES MACPHERSON (1736–1796)
From: *Ossian*

Long before these lines were ever put to paper, the ancients were paying their own kinds of homage to the sun and, in the process, endowing the literature of folklore with a variety of memorable passages. People of that time credited the sun's blazing presence with godlike powers. For some, it was the possession of a major deity. To the Egyptians, for instance, it was the giant ship in which the sun god Ra carried the dead across the "azure sea" of the sky to their final resting place. The Greeks said it was the blazing chariot driven by the handsome Helios Apollo.

Others believed it to be the eye of their premier gods — a power that saw all and knew all. It was the eye of Ahuranamazda in Persia; of Varuna in India; and of the supreme deity of Africa's Bushmen. The Samoyeds of Russia conceived the sun and the moon as the eyes of heaven, with the former being the eye for good, and the latter for evil; thus, for the Samoyeds, as for the peoples of several other cultures, the sun and moon symbolized the two polarities in the world of morality.

Still other cultures looked on the sun as a god itself. Several thought of it as a deity that traveled the sky by day and passed beneath the earth by night, there to illumine the region of the dead. To the Japanese and the Peruvian Incas, the sun was the celestial ancestor from whom their rulers descended. Many Indian peoples of the western hemisphere — from the Crow, Zuni, Cherokee, and Apache of North America to the Aztecs of Mexico and southward to the Incas — worshiped it as their supreme god, feeling that it was the giver and withholder of life. It brought the light that made work possible. When its mood was gentle, it gave fair weather that nourished the people, their crops, and their livestock. But, when it blazed too hot, it destroyed, scorching the earth, withering crops and forage, and burning people and animals alike with a killing dryness and thirst.

As they did with their other gods, the ancients sought to flatter and keep the sun happy by honoring it with temples, rituals, and dances. The dances, usually imitations of the sun's daily or yearly passage, often embraced more than an appeal for a general kindness; they were performed in thanksgiving for a good harvest, in hopes of a successful war, and as a plea for the end of an illness. The Aztecs each year, in a bid to make certain that the sun never destroyed them by abandoning its daily journey, selected a handsome young man to represent their sun god, Tezcatlipoca (meaning "Smoking Mirror"). The youth was treated with reverence throughout the year, after which he was sacrificed.

In most early cultures, the sun was thought of as male — and its nighttime counterpart, the moon, as female. The choice was made for reasons that must strike most moderns as blatantly chauvinistic. The sun was courageous, heroic; it blazed; it radiated an unquestionable strength; it was a force that could give or take away life: all male attributes in the ancient mind. But the moon was quiet, serene, and passive: characteristics seen as distinctly female.

Depending on one's turn of mind, these many and various ancient views are fictions that can be anything from quaint to outrageous (as in the case of the Aztecs). But we must concede one point here. Those of our distant forebears who saw the sun as a giver of life and a vital force in the making of our weather were right on the mark. The only difference is that they guessed at the reasons; we today know the facts of the matter.

To avoid stumbling into a thicket of scientific complexities, let us settle for a general statement about the sun as a giver of life. Energy is the force that drives life; without it, life would cease. The earth receives almost all of its energy from the sun. We also take some energy from the heat generated at the earth's core, from tidal actions induced (in the main) by the moon, from the distant stars, and from such radioactive terrestrial elements as uranium and plutonium. But these energies are nothing when compared to that provided by the sun. And what of the sun as a vital force in the creation of our weather? Before we can deal with this question, we need to take a close look at the sun and its relationship to the earth.

SUN AND EARTH

Considering the sun's importance to us, it always comes as something of a surprise, even in this age of widespread scientific sophistication, to remember that it is just one of countless stars in the universe — and a small one at that, being of less than normal star size. But, though formally classed as a dwarf, it's a giant as far as we are concerned. Its diameter, measuring about 840,000 miles, is 109 times greater than the earth's at the equator — 7,926.41 miles. The sun's volume stands at 1.3 million times that of the earth, and its mass is estimated to be 33,000 times greater.

Listed by astronomers as a yellow star, the sun has been described as an endless nuclear explosion. Known to contain more than sixty elements found on earth (with all of them in a gaseous state because of the awesome heat), it is an ever-pulsating mass of electromagnetic matter, with its interior temperatures estimated to run in excess of 36,000,000°F., and its surface temperatures at about 10,000°F. From its writhing surface, various rays (radio, infrared, visible, ultraviolet, X-rays, and gamma) radiate into space and bombard the earth.

However, the energy that reaches earth is but a fraction of the sun's total output. Most of the rays are lost in space; some travel to our fellow planets, some are deflected and returned to space by our clouds. Yet, minute as it is, the energy received is vital to our survival and the creation of our weather.

The heat that is generated by the sun's energy can be tremendous, as we've all learned on a summer's afternoon, a fact that British writer Sydney Smith noted in memorable fashion:

> *"Heat, ma'am!" I said: "it was so dreadful that I found there was nothing left for it but to take off my flesh and sit in my bones."*
>
> — From: *Lady Holland's Memoir*

Were it not for a reciprocal terrestrial and atmospheric action, that heat would be enough to scorch the earth barren. On receiving the energy, the earth and the atmosphere radiate a percentage of it back out and thus safeguard us from a lethal baking. In general, the earth and the objects on it absorb about 47% of the arriving energy. Roughly 36% is reflected back into space as heat, with an additional 17% absorbed by the atmosphere and clouds before ever reaching earth.

There was a time when humankind, in one of its various but understandable pomposities (understandable because the facts of the matter were yet unknown), thought that the earth stood at the center of the universe and was circled by the sun and moon. But, with the works of Greece's Aristarchus (circa 310–230 B.C.) and, centuries later, Poland's Copernicus (1473–1543), the truth began to emerge — that, while the moon circles us, we and the moon and the other planets in our solar system orbit the sun. Today, we know that our own orbit carries us along an elliptical path that brings us to within varying distances of the sun. When our orbit is at perihelion, we are closest to the sun — about 91.5 million miles from its blazing surface. At aphelion, we are farthest away — some 94.5 million miles distant. The average distance between the sun and earth stands at 92.96 million miles.

Our orbit carries us once around the sun every 365 days, 5 hours, 48 minutes, and 46 seconds. Once based on the passage of the moon, our calendar is now fashioned on the solar orbit. The elapsed time of this orbit gives us a much simpler measure on which to base the length of our years than does the lunar cycle of 29½ days from new moon to new moon. As was noted in the nineteenth century:

> *Whether we wake or we sleep,*
> *Whether we carol or weep,*
> *The sun and his Planets in chime,*
> *Marketh the going of time.*

— EDWARD FITZGERALD (1809–1883)
From: *Chronomoros*

The earth spins on its axis as it travels, making one complete revolution through day and night every 24 hours. Our solar calendar aligns itself as closely as possible with the elapsed orbital time by using a 365-day year. But, to account for the approximate quarter-day of extra time consumed by the orbit and to bring things into better alignment, the calendar must periodically include an additional day. It does so by adding a day to February every four years — except at the change of the century — and giving us a leap year. (To maintain the alignment, however, there must be a leap year at the change of every fourth century. The rapidly approaching year 2000 will be a leap year.) As we spin along, we do so on a tilted axis — a tilt of 23.5° to the plane of our orbit. It is this cant that, as we'll see momentarily, gives us our seasons, bringing them to the northern hemisphere at one time of year, and to the southern half of the globe at another.

SUN AND WEATHER

Temperature, pressure, moisture, and wind: these are the atmospheric ingredients necessary for the creation of our weather. The sun's heat is the force that sets them in motion, mixes them, and, as a consequence, enables them to exhibit their many behaviors.

In the coming chapters, we'll see the various phenomena — the winds, the clouds, the rains and snows, the sky colors, the rainbows, the dews and frosts, the thunderstorms — that result from the action-reaction pattern engendered by the sun, earth, and atmosphere. For the present, we need only talk about a few basic solar facts. We'll begin with our seasons.

THE TILT OF THE EARTH *as it travels around the sun gives us our seasons. Reading counterclockwise from the top right, the seasons are winter, spring, summer, and autumn.*

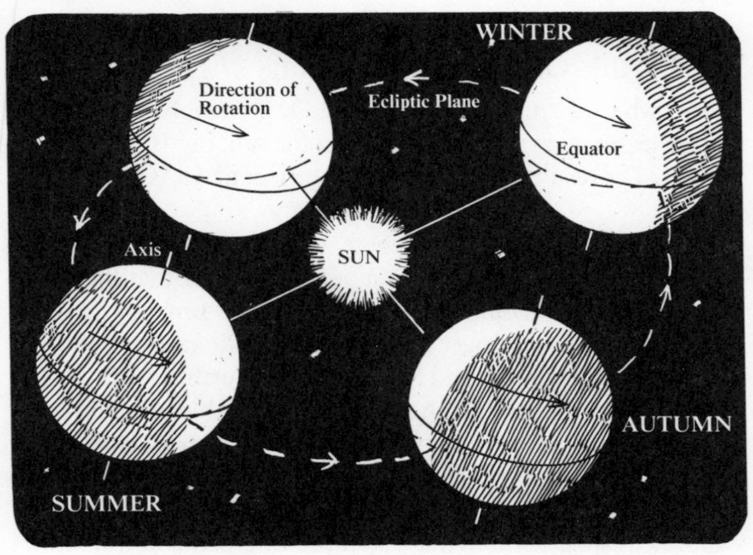

The Seasons

The sun combines with the earth's tilt to generate a month-by-month change in the amount of solar radiation reaching us. That change carries us routinely from season to season each year.

Many people think that the shape of the earth's orbit is responsible for our seasons. They reason that summer must come when the earth is closest to the sun and receiving the full benefit of its heat, and winter arrives when the earth is farthest away. Actually, the earth is at aphelion (its greatest distance from the sun) during our northern hemisphere summers, and at perihelion (its closest distance) during our winters. Accounting for this is the earth's tilt toward the sun during our midyear months, and away from it during our late- and early-year months.

The exact reverse applies in the southern hemisphere, when at midyear, the tilt is away from the sun and winter is at hand. In the late- and early-year months, the earth leans toward the sun and summer occurs.

The Earth's Orbit and the Seasons

And what of spring and autumn? Quite simply, the earth is neither leaning toward nor away from the sun, but is tilting off to the side. The result: less heat than in summer and less cold than in winter.

Here in the northern hemisphere, sunlight pours in across the North Pole during the summer months, meaning that the sun is riding higher above our horizons than at other times of the year. Hence, the days are longer and provide additional hours for the solar radiation to strike and heat the earth. Further, with the sun more directly overhead, each ray of sunlight is able to concentrate itself on a small area and create a heat of greater intensity. The same applies to the southern hemisphere when, in its summer, the sunlight falls across the South Pole.

Our hemispheric tilt in the winter prevents sunlight from flow-

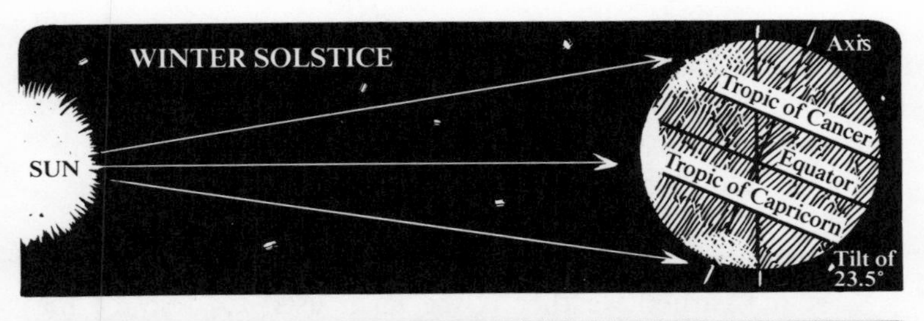

When the northern hemisphere is tilted away from the sun, we have our winter season; when tilted toward the sun, we have our summer season.

ing in across the North Pole. At its northernmost point, the light reaches a latitude short of the Pole. The sun, then, rides lower to our horizons, shortening the days and allowing less time for a heat build-up. Further, the individual rays do not strike the earth as directly as in the summer months. Coming in at a slant, each, with a consequent loss in heat intensity, must spread itself over a greater area.

The Winds

Our planet is an oblate spheroid. Its circumference, of course, is greatest at its center — its equatorial region — and then narrows steadily in either direction to the North and South Poles. Because of the earth's shape and axial tilt, throughout the year the equatorial region receives a greater share of solar radiation than do our other areas. The air there is greatly heated and, as a consequence, rises, expands, and sweeps away to the north and south — and the world's winds are born.

Chapter Four will deal with the complex actions that take shape when those winds encounter such factors as the earth's contours, its lands and waters, and its daily rotation on its axis.

Climate

As stated earlier, weather is the term used to describe the momentary or day-to-day behaviors of the atmosphere at any point on the earth's surface. Climate, on the other hand, is the average type of weather routinely enjoyed or suffered, year after year, by a given area. The sun and our axial tilt combine to help give the earth its various climates (the winds also play a major role here). The equatorial region and the areas to its immediate north and south have warm to hot climates because they consistently receive a heavier and more direct concentration of the sun's rays. On the other hand, the polar regions are cold because, even

When the air above the land is heated, it rises and allows cool air to move in and replace it. The sea air arrives as a refreshing breeze or wind.

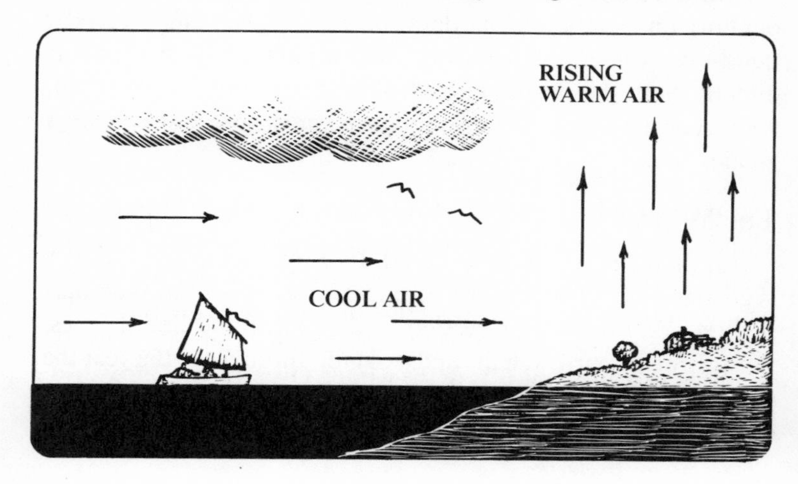

in summer, the sun is striking them at a slant and, in winter, is touching them only slightly or not at all.

Two other factors join the sun in producing climates — the rates at which its heat is absorbed and then radiated back into the atmosphere by land and water. The two rates differ, with the land doing a faster job of absorption and release than does the water, which lags well behind. Responsible for the gap is the fact that the land accepts heat only to a depth of a few inches before thrusting it back out. The ocean takes in heat to a depth of 80 feet or more, with its movement often thrusting it even deeper.

This difference in the absorption and radiation rates usually causes the interiors of continents to have hotter summers and colder winters than do sea islands and continental coasts. Here's how the difference shows itself along a coast: the air above the land, heating more quickly than the sea air during the daytime hours, rises more quickly than its counterpart. The cooler sea air moves in to fill the space left open and arrives in the form of a refreshing breeze or wind. At night, the land quickly releases its heat, with the heat then rapidly cooling in the atmosphere. The slower-acting sea air, now the warmer of the two, rises, and the cool land air drops in to replace it. The seasiders are blessed with another refreshing breeze or wind. Seamen have long noted this phenomenon:

> *In by day,*
> *Out by night.*

Further, the difference in the land-sea rates causes ocean areas and their islands to react slowly to seasonal changes. Usually, they trail one to two months behind the continents in their seasonal transitions. Finally, the range between summer and winter land temperatures is far greater than that of their sea counterparts. The land can witness striking changes — from over 100°F. in the summer to well below 0°F. in the winter. Over most of the world's ocean areas, there is usually no more than an 18° difference between the summer and winter temperatures.

THE SUN AS FORECASTER

With their varied and imaginative views of the sun, the ancients gave the literature of weather lore some of its most fascinating pages. The same, of course, must be said of all those observers who, from ancient times onward, looked to the sun for clues to the coming weather. Some thought it to be a flawless predictor:

> *Above the rest, the sun who never lies,*
> *Foretells the changes of weather in the skies.*

> *The sun reveals the secrets of the sky;*
> *And who dares give the source of light the lie.*

These comments are from the pen of the Roman poet Virgil and appear in his *Georgics,* a work that, dedicated to extolling the virtues of the rustic life and its outdoor labor, also gives attention to weather topics. Both statements are true, provided a limitation is placed on them. If a sun prediction is to work, it should be based on the assorted complexions — ranging from fiery red to gold and on to a pale gray — that the sun takes on when certain atmospheric conditions play upon its face. These tints are excellent forecasters of the weather to come in the immediate future — in the next hours or days.

As often as not down through the centuries, the sun has been victimized by forecasts that have had nothing to do with tint and that can only be described, at best, as misguided. Believed to this day in many areas, they've concerned themselves with the idea that the sun's presence on a given day guarantees its appearance on another given day or promises a certain kind of weather. As are so many of the world's erroneous ideas, they are both interesting and entertaining.

The Mistaken

> *If it is sunny and fair on the first Sunday in the month, every Sunday but one in the month will be sunny and fair.*

or conversely:

> *If it storms on the first Sunday of the month, it will storm every Sunday in the month.*
>
> — OLD CIRCUS SAYING
>
> (Oddly enough, circus people claim that a tracking of this proverb at one time showed it to be valid about 90% of the time over a 10-year period.)

> *There is never a Saturday without sun.*

> *The sun shines every Saturday but one in the year.*
>
> — BOSTON SAYING

And, with a lovely Latin ring to it, this one from Spain:

> *No Saturday without sun, no girl without love.*

These prophecies simply do not work at all times but only on occasion. It is significant that they all refer to days of religious import for generations of people. Sunday has long been the day of rest and religious observance for most Christians, while Saturday was — and, for Judaism, still is — the Sabbath day; further, for the Christians of medieval Europe, Saturday was celebrated as the Virgin Mary's Day. Devout souls could not help thinking of one or the other of the days as having to be especially blessed so far as the weather was concerned. Out of such a view — and, undoubtedly, out of occasional good Saturday weathers that were then cast in the "stone of proverb" as universals — came prophecies that, though obviously invalid, continue to be widely believed today.

But there is one troublesome aspect to the predictions. Though we logically know them to be without merit, they can be devils when it comes to disproving them. So long as some gleams of sunlight break through on a Saturday or Sunday — no matter how weak, short-lived, or watery they may be — some people will continue to consider the proverbs as valid.

Not all the sun predictions having to do with days of religious observance are on the happy side. Widely considered in meteorological circles to be just as false as the above — but just as much cherished by countless non-scientific believers — are these old forecasts of the trouble that lies ahead when the sun appears on one of the year's coldest and often bleakest days in the northern hemisphere:

> *If Candlemas be fair and clear,*
> *Two winters will you have this year.*

> *Just as far as the sun shines in on Candlemas Day,*
> *Just so far will the snow blow in before May.*

> *A bright, clear Candlemas means a late spring.*

Candlemas Day is celebrated on February 2 and, in the United States, traditionally wins national press coverage for the humble groundhog (or, in the Southwest, for "Agua Fria Freddie," the sidewinder). Out of his den he comes that day for a peek at the weather. If there is enough sun at hand to cause him to cast a shadow, he tarries for a moment and then scuttles back into his winter quarters — and, to us, this is a sign that winter is to hang about for at least another 6 weeks, giving us "two winters," "snow in before May," or a "late spring."

So far as meteorologists are concerned, the whole idea is a pleasant nonsense. Many of them argue that the groundhog's retreat is likely caused by the fact that, after weeks spent in the dark, his eyes are pained by the sunlight. He seeks the only relief available to him: returning underground. It makes good sense. Yet as is so often the fate of good sense, it has done nothing to spoil everyone's February fun. But it's quite possible that the meteorologists are wrong, quite possible that the Candlemas prediction is neither a falsehood nor a pleasant nonsense. One thing is certain. What was seen on Candlemas Day was anything but pleasant nonsense to the European farmers of yesteryear. Depending on the area, the stars of the day were usually bears or badgers. They were watched closely, and if there was anything that the nervous farmers did not want to see, it was shadow-inducing sunlight.

Why? Farmers have always considered the first three months of the year to be critical to a plentiful harvest of their fruits, vegetables, and winter grains. For best results, the winter had to advance through these months to a gentle end, producing a slow and steady thaw. Dreaded was the sudden appearance of unseasonably warm spells. They caused a premature thawing that would likely be followed by a cold snap — a "second winter" — that would refreeze, damage, and even kill the developing crops.

February, falling in the middle of the vital 3-month period, was considered especially crucial to the welfare of the plantings. Hence, a sunny Candlemas Day became one of the most feared of weather signs. Actually, farmers had looked on February as a critical month for centuries before the Candlemas tradition took shape. The tradition itself — the designation of February 2 as the key day for judging the coming weather — was a Christian innovation. The day celebrates the purification of the Virgin Mary. Over the years since its birth, it has inspired many a forecast, including the following four, all of which come from Great Britain:

If Candlemas Day be mild and gay,
Go saddle your horses and buy them hay.
If Candlemas Day be stormy and black,
It carries the winter away on its back.

If Candlemas Day is cloudy and black,
It always hugs winter away on its back.

If Candlemas Day is fair and bright,
Winter will take another flight.
If Candlemas Day bring storm and rain,
Winter is gone and will not come again.

In Yorkshire ancient people say
If February's second day
Be very fair and clear,
It doth portend a scanty year
For hay and grass, but if it rains
They never then perplex their brains.

Additionally, there are what may well be the three grimmest forecasts in weather lore, speaking as they do of the economic disaster that a warm February can bring to the farm and pasture:

The Welshman had rather see his dam [wife]
on the bier
Than see a fair Februeer.

On Candlemas Day, if the sun shines clear,
The shepherd had rather see his wife on the bier.

The shepherd would rather see the wolf enter his
flock than see the sun on Candlemas Day.

The Valid

> *For oft we find him* [the sun] *finishing his race,*
> *With various colors erring on his face.*

— VIRGIL
From: *Georgics*

In turning to the valid folk predictions, we come to those based on the sun's complexion as varying conditions in the atmosphere play upon its face. The colors that you need to watch for here are red, gray, gold, and brass, with the first two being especially fine forecasters of rain:

> *If the sun in red should set,*
> *The next day will surely be wet.*
> *If the sun should set in gray,*
> *The next will be a rainy day.*

Though they can be on view at other times of the day, the red and gray hues are most often seen at dawn and sunset. This is because sunlight, white to begin with, is split into the colors of the spectrum as it passes through the atmosphere and ricochets off the water vapor and foreign particles there — dust, smoke, and such. The splitting is most evident at dawn and sunset because the sun is lowest to the horizon then and is casting its rays through the thickest concentration of atmosphere. The presence of some shade of red suggests an atmosphere heavily laden with dust and smoke, so heavily laden that only the sun's longest light wavelengths — those at the red end of the spectrum — can break through, with those of shorter wavelengths being broken up. A heavy concentration of dust and smoke suggests dry air, but the opening lines of the proverb promise a wet day to come. What is at stake here is the fact that the presence of moisture intensifies the red hue. The heavier the moisture content, the deeper and more fiery will be the red. Hence, when a deep red is on hand at sunset — and that's the shade to which the proverb is referring — the sun is being seen through an atmosphere heavy with moisture that lies between us and its descent in the west. Because the winds in our latitudes flow principally from some point in the west, we can expect them to bring the wet air and its rain to us within the next hours. (A caution: at first glance, the red sun proverb seems to be related to the collection of very familiar sayings and rhymes having to do with the color of the sky, principally the collection made up of the "red sky at night" prophecies, all of which promise not rain but fair weather. Don't let this apparent contradiction confuse you. There is a relationship here because the red sky group deals with the same color and the same time of day, but it is a slight one. As we'll see in Chapter Six, the red sky proverbs involve a different shade of red.)

Gray also indicates an atmosphere heavily laden with moisture — and painted over with darkish, rain-threatening clouds. Our westerly winds will more than likely bring rain sometime in the night or by the next day.

What is promised by the sun's gray look, and the foreboding sky that makes it, did not escape the notice of William Shakespeare:

> *The sun sets weeping in the lowly west,*
> *Witnessing storms to come, woe and unrest.*

Nor did it escape the notice of many an American farmer:

> *If you see the sun set in a cloud, it will rain tomorrow.*

While it can be looked on as a rule-of-thumb truth, the proverb is trustworthy only when the cloud is a large one. A small cloud that happens to get in the way of the sun means only that it has gotten in the way of the sun. Further, if you were to change your viewing position by even a few city blocks, you'd likely find that the cloud is no longer covering the sun and that the sunset sky is perfectly clear.

Now, since we've mentioned a clear sky, let's spend a moment with a golden — or bright-faced — sun at day's end. Its complexion indicates dry atmospheric conditions approaching from the west with the wind. And so we have:

> *When the sun sets bright and clear,*
> *An easterly wind you need not fear.*

(While our weather comes generally from the west in our latitudes, a storm is often accompanied by east winds. Chapter Four will discuss this point in detail.)

When we turn our attention to the dawn, we find that weather watchers through the centuries have disliked a red sun here quite as much as at nightfall — and for the same reason. The sun is shining through moist air that is close by or directly overhead and the threat of rain is at hand:

> *If red the sun begin his race,*
> *Be sure the rain will fall apace.*
> *In fiery red the sun doth rise,*
> *Then wades through clouds to mount the skies.*

> *A gaudy morning bodes a wet afternoon.*

And this antique specimen of bigotry:

> *A morning sun, and a wine-bred child, and*
> *a Latin-bred woman seldom end well.*

And a blunt American way of assessing matters:

> *Friday dawns clear as a bell,*
> *Rain on Sunday, sure as hell.*

Though the red and gray hues are most often seen at sunset, they can also be on view throughout the day, as indicated by this age-old proverb:

> *A red sun has water in his eye.*

We come now to a final note on the sun's appearance and what it forbodes:

> *When the sun sets unhappy, the morning will be angry with storms.*
>
> — AMERICAN INDIAN SAYING

> *The paleness of the pilot is a sign of storm.*

> *If the sun goes pale to bed,*
> *'Twill rain tomorrow, it is said.*

The terms "unhappy" and "pale" refer to the veiled, shimmering look that the sun sometimes assumes. That look, often one shade of gray or another, means that the sun is being viewed through moist air and high-riding clouds that are likely arriving in the vanguard of rain-bearing clouds.

* * *

At this point, we'll turn to the sun's replacement — sometimes pale, sometimes brilliantly luminous, the moon is seen only because it reflects the sunlight in which it has been bathed since the birth of the universe. It may depend on the sun's light for its visibility, but it is quite the sun's equal in the pages of folklore.

CHAPTER THREE

A Sky of Moon and Moonlight

CIRCLING US while we orbit the sun, and reflected to our eyes by the light of the sun, the moon is a satellite of the earth. However, it is large enough relative to the earth's size for the two of them to be widely considered not a planet and satellite but a double planet. The moon's diameter measures 2,159.9 miles in comparison to the earth's equatorial diameter of 7,926.41 miles. It is believed that the two planets were formed simultaneously.

The moon's orbit carries it along an elliptical path that causes its distance from the earth to vary. At apogee — its greatest distance from the earth — it is 252,710 miles away; at perigee — its closest distance — 221,463 miles. The mean distance between the centers of the earth and moon runs to 238,860 miles.

Rotating on its axis as it travels, the moon completes a circuit of the earth in about 27½ days in reference to the stars, and in about 29½ days in reference to the sun. Accounting for the two-day difference is the fact that both the earth and moon are in orbit. Of the two circuits, the longer revolution has a greater import for us.

It causes those 29½ days (or, to be specific, 29 days, 12 hours, and 44.05 minutes) to elapse from the time we see one new moon until we see the next.

But the shorter revolution is also significant, because the moon rotates on its axis in an amount of time exactly equal to this circuit: 27.321666 days. The rates of the rotation and the circuit cause the moon to show the same side of itself — the same "face" — to us year after year. It was not until 1959, when the unmanned but camera-equipped Russian space vehicle Lunik III orbited the moon, that we gained any real idea of what the hidden side of that distant satellite looked like. Since then, photographs of virtually all of the moon's surface have been taken and transmitted to earth by U.S. lunar probes.

The moon oscillates, and in tandem with certain other factors, this oscillation permits us to see more than the face of the moon. At one time or another in the course of a year, six-tenths of the moon's surface are visible: "extended" stretches of the lunar surface along its east and west edges and along its north and south curves. The other four-tenths of the surface remain perennially out of our sight.

As it makes its 29½-day journey around the earth, the moon passes through a cycle consisting of two major steps — waxing and waning. The cycle begins with the new moon, a time when the moon is fully dark because it is lying between the earth and the sun. When the moon begins to wax, increasingly larger areas of its surface are illuminated by the sun and become visible. The waxing takes us through a first-quarter stage to the quarter moon and then on through a second quarter to the full moon, when the entire face is on spectacular view. The waning period begins immediately, with the visible surface growing steadily smaller, passing through the third and fourth stages, until the moon is again between the sun and earth, cutting off all illumination and bringing the return of the new moon. The moon is crescent-

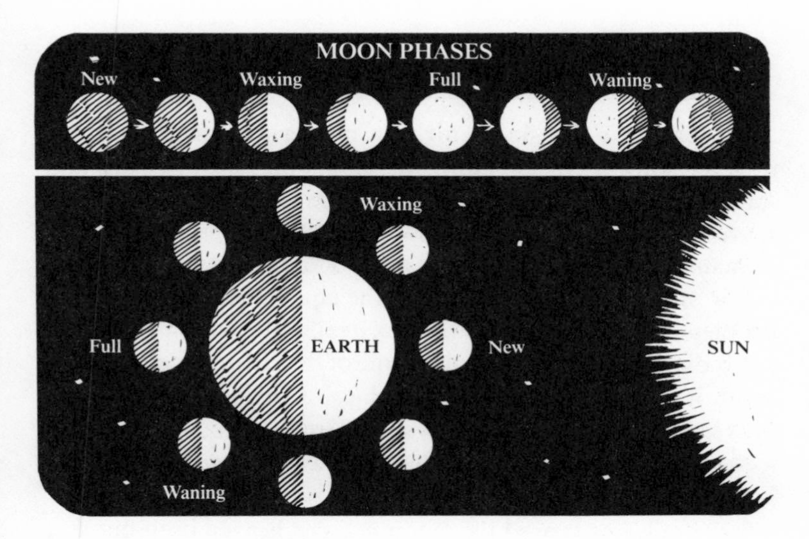

THE PHASES OF THE MOON.

shaped during much of its passage across the sky, a shape that, as we will see, has played a major role in lunar superstition and weather lore.

Working together as they travel around a common center of gravity (which is located within the earth), the moon and earth send a bulge — a tidal rise and fall — moving along our planet's surface. This tidal action, which results from a combination of centrifugal force and the moon's gravitational pull, occurs on both our water and land surfaces. It is most clearly seen in our waters and, though undeniably present, is almost undetectable on our lands. The rise and fall occur on most points of the earth every 12.42 hours. They are at their greatest when the moon is new or full, and at their lowest during the moon's first and third quarters.

THE MOON: EARLY BELIEFS

Suspended in the sky at night (a mysterious and frightening time to many ancients), luminous, sometimes deathly pale, and sometimes a glowing, virginal white, the moon has been a rich source of myth, symbolism, and superstition ever since the day humans first began looking at it and pondering its significance.

For many early cultures, it was the equivalent to our heaven. Peoples as widely separated as the Greeks, Persians, and American Indians believed it to be the home of the virtuous departed. In India, it was not only the resting place of the dead but also the light shed by that country's ancestors. Greek legend held that the souls who lived there dispatched oracles earthward to advise humankind.

Some cultures viewed the moon not as a heaven itself but as a vehicle that carried the dead to their final resting place. In pre-Christian Europe, for instance, the Gnostics looked on it as the ship that carried departed souls to the sun; the concept of the moon as a ship was obviously derived from its crescent shape during waxing and waning.

Other cultures, however, developed more pessimistic theories. The Slavic belief was that the sinful dead ended up on the moon. Elsewhere in Europe, legend spoke of it as a storehouse for all the human possibilities for good that had been squandered on earth. Delivered and deposited there were the likes of broken promises, empty emotional upheavals, greedy acts, lusts, cheatings, and wasted time.

Early on, the moon was given a godly rank or was revered as a force with godlike powers. It was worshiped for its coolness and gentleness in those countries where the sun burned the earth dry and barren. Other ancients conceived of it as the force that awakened and massed the stars. Of an unhappy turn of mind were the early Finno-Ugric peoples — the Finns, Lapps, Bulgarians, Hungarians, and Estonians — who saw the moon as an old man with an evil eye.

In its godly capacity, the moon was variously depicted as a male, a bisexual, and a female. It seems to have been primarily regarded as a male, then patriarchal societies transformed it into a female, demoting it in rank and elevating the sun to the position of the pre-eminent god or collection of gods. Much behind the demotion, as was mentioned in Chapter Two, was the moon's passivity, which struck the ancient male mind as characteristically feminine. Also playing a part was the moon's monthly waxing-and-waning cycle. Occurring regularly as it does, it was felt to have a mysterious but seemingly obvious connection with the woman's physiological cycle.

In time, as god, goddess, or major natural force, the endlessly circling moon came to symbolize many, if not all, aspects of life on earth. Its cycle — from dark to luminous, and then from luminous back to dark — was seen as representing the span of human, animal, and plant life; the biological and intellectual changes in the maturing individual; and the separation of good (luminosity) and evil (darkness), and of the superior and the inferior. This last concept is especially evident in the old Greek view of the moon as two goddesses — the infernal Hecate before moonrise and after moonset, and the celestial Artemis when the moon was visible.

Its cycling, ending always in darkness but returning always with a growing luminosity, also suggested to many ancients the idea of reincarnation — that life itself was an unending process that was not closed with death but only begun again. Death was but a transitory state, a modifying pause before life, and like the reappearing moon, was born again. Emerging here in a number of cultures was the belief that the dead not only traveled to the moon but also returned from it at a later time. The Greek biographer and philosopher Plutarch (circa A.D. 46–120) had this idea in mind when he wrote that the virtuous were sent to the moon to have their souls purified, after which their spirits were sent on to the sun and their bodies were returned to the earth.

The cycling seemed of such import that the moon was said to control the flow of the seasons; to determine the growth and eventual decomposition of organisms; and to govern (as is the truth of the matter) the tides.

Until the Industrial Revolution began some two hundred years ago, the world's societies were agrarian in nature. The lunar cycle, which was used to calculate the passage of time long before the solar calendar was developed, was seen as vital to the livelihood of the people. Dependable in its monthly passage, the cycle came to serve as a guidepost for the planting and nurturing of crops, with many farmers today in all parts of the globe continuing to swear by it. As an agricultural guide, it gave birth to such general advice as the following:

> *Always plant your seeds by the full of the moon.*

> *Always plant your beans when the moon is old.*
> *Then they won't run to vines.*

But —

> *Set out the slips for your house plants when the*
> *moon is new in August. The plants will thrive.*

And such rhymed advice as:

> *Go plant the bean when the moon is light,*
> *And you will find that this is right.*
> *Plant the potatoes when the moon is dark,*
> *And to this line you always hark.*
> *But if you vary this rule,*
> *You will find you are a fool.*
> *If you follow this rule to the end,*
> *You will always have money to spend.*

All such advice has long been the subject of controversy between meteorologists and farmers. The former contend that a planting's welfare has nothing to do with the moon, but with soil conditions, the amount of annual freezing, and a gradual spring thaw. As for planting by the full moon, the meteorological opinion is that the practice came about because the bright illumination helped the early farmers to see better what they were doing. But don't try to convince many of today's farmers of this, for like their counterparts in the past, they swear that full-of-the-moon plantings send out deeper roots.

The same will happen when you challenge many a modern on yet another matter — the superstitions that have grown up around the moon.

MOON SUPERSTITIONS: TODAY

Regardless of how advanced beyond the ancients we may think ourselves to be, we've never completely broken with the past. We've abandoned the idea of a moon goddess, yes, and have landed on the moon to learn the truth of things there, but like it or not, we're still quite as superstitious as our most distant forebears. For proof, just look to a few of the quaint beliefs that have been passed down to us through the centuries and that are still widely accepted today, sometimes seriously, sometimes in the spirit of good fun, and sometimes with the simple (and ancient) thought of not wanting to take chances with fate:

> *If you wish on a new moon, your wish will come true.*

> *Turn your money over when you see a new moon. It will bring you more money.*

> *Jingle the money in your pocket on seeing a new moon. You will have money until the next new moon comes.*

> *Make sure that your first glimpse of the new moon is always from over your right shoulder, for then you will have good luck. Bad luck will come if you look over your left shoulder.*

Likewise, make certain that the new moon is not directly in front of you when first you see it; otherwise, you're bound for some sort of a fall — perhaps physical, perhaps from grace. In rhyme, this superstition is voiced as:

> *Moon in the face,*
> *Open disgrace.*

Recite the rhyme:

> *I see the moon, the moon sees me.*
> *The moon sees somebody I want to see.*

Now say the name of the one you wish to see. In a day or two, that person will appear.

> *To have new work prosper, begin it with the new moon.*

> *Have your hair cut at new moon and it will grow out much better. The same goes for beards.*

These are all old ideas that have refused to go away. They're quaint and certainly fun to read. And who knows? With each promising a fine reward for but a moment of your time, they might be worth a try. After all, even some of the most skeptical of our lot will agree that the things that eventually come true in life are the things we believe will come true.

THE MOON AND THE WEATHER

> *But chiefly look to Cynthia's varying face;*
> *There surest signs of coming weather trace.*
>
> — ARATUS (circa 315–245 B.C.)

Though Rome's Virgil thought that the sun, "above the rest," never lied when foretelling "the changes of weather in the skies," the Greek poet Aratus placed his trust in the moon, as did the composers of these two old saws:

> *If a crescent moon hangs like a cradle* [on its back]
> *in the springtime, the summer will be dry.*

> *If you see a bright star behind a crescent moon, you*
> *will have rain and snow. If the star is in front or*
> *within the crescent, you will have fair weather.*

It is generally agreed that the two sayings are false. But the question of whether Aratus was justified in his faith has long been a subject of debate. Still asked today is the question: does the moon, which has always been so influential in human thinking, likewise influence our weather?

On two counts, the answer might seem to be "yes." First, it seems likely that the moon exerts a physiological and psychological effect on the human constitution. Many people have long equated the incidence and severity of illness with the moon, with Shakespeare noting, in *A Midsummer Night's Dream,* that the moon "pale in her anger, washes all the air" so that "rheumatic diseases do abound." Some early cultures forbade their people to look at the moon for fear that it would blind them or otherwise damage their eyes; others regarded the final waning to darkness as a signal of a death in the village; and, of course, there was the widespread conviction that the cycle of the moon was related to the woman's physiological cycle with its many discomforts.

As for the emotions, it's a well-established police fact that the rate of violent crime often goes up at full moon. Countless drivers are more than convinced that their fellow motorists have the habit of pulling the silliest of stunts during the same period. The Eskimos of Greenland may have noted some form of the same peculiarities; perhaps as an outgrowth of the suspected connection between the moon and the female cycle, they held that the moon incited their women to orgies. They ordered them never to look at it for more than an instant or so. Foolish behaviors at full moon have been noted for so long by so many that, centuries ago, the word "lunar" was expanded to "lunatic."

All this being the case, it seems reasonable to ask: if the moon can play such havoc on the world's people, then what's to stop it from influencing the world's weather?

On the second count, look to the tides and their awesome rise and fall of countless tons of water. Since they are much the work of the moon (and, to a lesser degree, the sun), does it not indicate that the moon also has the power to affect the weather? Generations of seafarers have certainly thought it does. They early noted that storms often come with high tides.

Meteorologists, however, have long contended that, unlike the sun, the moon has little or no effect on our weather. Some agree that the moon does seem to exert an effect on the human physiological and emotional system, but wonder if this is a psychological bequest from centuries ago when humankind stood in awe and fear of the moon's ghostly look and repeated appearances. As for a storm-tide connection, science now says (as we'll see in

Chapter Six) that a pre-storm condition — a drop in air pressure — reduces the atmospheric weight holding the water down and allows it to rise and hit a coastline with higher than usual tides. It's a case then of the tides coming with the storm rather than the other way around.

Science thinks so little of the moon's exertions on the weather that many weather texts mention it only in passing, while others take no notice of it at all. In general, the traditional meteorological attitude can be summed up in this verse from the 19th century:

The moon and the weather
May change together;
But change of the moon
Does not change the weather.

If we'd no moon at all,
And that may seem strange,
We still should have weather
That's subject to change.

But, mind you, we're talking here about the traditional meteorological view. It's an outlook that may be subject to change. A New York University computer study done in the early 1960s with a half-century's worth of National Weather Service rainfall data indicated that rain and snow are more than apt to fall within 3 days of the full moon, and that, at the moon's first and third quarters, dry weather is an above-average possibility.

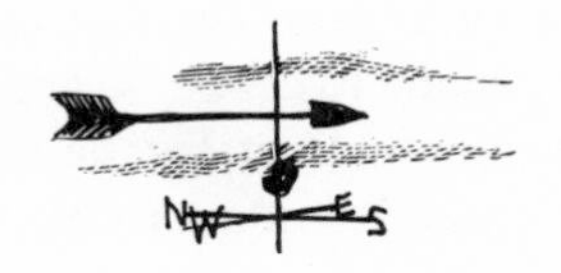

THE MOON AND PREDICTION

Whatever the truth may eventually — if ever — prove to be, the moon has prompted its fair share of folk weather predictions. For the most part, they unwittingly substantiate the traditional meteorological view. They are not built around lunar actions that can be thought of as influential. Rather, they concern themselves with the look of the moon as it hangs there in the sky.

For example, generations of farmers, seamen, scientists, and amateur forecasters have judged the coming weather on the moon's various "facial expressions" — its brightness, dimness, and sharpness. Others have based their predictions on its color, and still others on its shape. What they've all put into rhyme and proverb are the ways in which atmospheric actions affect the way we see the moon.

"Facial Expressions"

We'll begin with two aged but still widely respected sayings:

> *Clear moon,*
> *Frost soon.*

> *Moonlit nights have the heaviest frosts.*

The moon, of course, is clearly seen on nights that are themselves clear. They are also often cold nights. That combination brings a marked and steady decrease in the atmospheric temperature. In turn, the descending temperature causes water vapor in the air just above the ground to condense and appear as dew or — if the cold is severe enough — frost. In Chapter Seven, we'll talk in more detail of how dew and frost are formed.

The moon is also highly visible on clear, warm nights, a fact that accounts for the second line in the next proverb. But don't overlook the opening line, which talks of a change in the weather:

> *If the moon rises pale, expect rain.*
> *If it rises clear, expect fair.*

Or, to put matters more succinctly:

> *Pale moon doth rain.*

When the face of the moon pales — grows dull — we are seeing it through the high, thin clouds that customarily arrive in advance of heavy, rain-bearing clouds. Should the paleness develop over a period of several hours, the indications are that a warm front (see Chapter Four) and its rain are on the way. The thin clouds can appear miles ahead of the front, which moves lazily along at about 15 miles an hour or slower. On the basis of these two factors, it is usually estimated that rain can be expected in 12 to 14 hours after the dulling begins. Now to carry matters a step further:

> *When the moon loses its outline, rain can be*
> *expected in about 10 hours.*

While the prediction doesn't always work out, it is thought to be pretty reliable. What is happening is that those thin clouds, after having dulled the moon, are now being replaced by the heavier rain-bearing clouds, which are beginning to hide it from view. The front is closing in and the chances are good that it will arrive with its rain in the time stated.

Incidentally, the stars can also do a good job of forecasting when the air is filled with the pre-storm wet that dulls the moon. The atmosphere — humid, hazy, and increasingly cloudy — hides the smaller ones and blurs their brighter companions. As a result, we have:

> *When the stars begin to hide,*
> *Soon the rain will betide.*

And, because each bright star, blurred as it is, often gives the impression of being a small cluster of stars:

> *When the stars begin to huddle,*
> *The earth will soon become a puddle.*

A Change of Color

But back to the moon. Its color, in common with that of the sun, can be altered. In our American Southwest, the Zuni Indians long ago noted that a certain switch of color provided a clue to the future. It was the very same clue that a sun of the same shade gave. They had this to say:

> *The moon, her face if red be,*
> *Of water speaks she.*

The proverb has been joined through the centuries by various others. Beginning with the complete version of a proverb already mentioned, here are four examples famous among weather lorists:

> *Pale moon doth rain,*
> *Red moon doth blow,*
> *White moon doth neither rain nor snow.*

> *If on her cheeks you see the maiden's blush,*
> *The moon foreshows that winds will rush.*

— VIRGIL
From: *Georgics*

If three days old her face be bright and clear,
No rain or stormy gale the sailors fear;
But if she rise with bright and blushing cheek,
The blustering winds the bending masts will shake.

— Aratus

If the moon shows a silver shield,
Be not afraid to reap your field;
But if she rises haloed round,
Soon we'll tread on deluged ground.

As is true of the red sun, the "blushing" moon is being viewed through an atmosphere that, heavily laden with moisture, promises stormy weather with its usual accompanying winds. The "white," "bright and clear," or "silver shield" moon is visible on nights free of the pre-storm conditions. But look again at the third and fourth lines in the proverb above. They bring us to one of the most reliable of the moon's predictive powers.

The Halo Effect

When round the moon there is a brugh [halo],
The weather will be cold and rough.

For I fear a hurricane;
Last night the moon had a golden ring,
And tonight no moon we see.

— Henry W. Longfellow
From: "Wreck of the Hesperus"

The moon with a circle brings water in her beak.

A halo may be either an arc or a ring that, sometimes accompanied by an inner red band, takes shape when the moon's light is reflected off the ice crystals in the high-flying clouds that so often precede rain-bearing clouds. Its diameter is large to begin with and its size is constant, but it gives the impression of becoming even larger as the storm draws nearer; at the same time, it seems to retreat deeper into space. All this is an optical phenomenon that occurs when the moonlight begins to reflect off the storm's actual rain-bearing clouds as, heavy and dark, they move in and descend to lower altitudes. As a consequence, we have these time-honored forecasts:

> *When the wheel is far,*
> *The storm is na'r.*
> *When the wheel is na'r,*
> *The storm is far.*

> *Near burr* [halo],
> *Far rain.*

> *The bigger the ring,*
> *The nearer the wet.*

And then we have:

> *When there is a circle around the moon, count the stars within the circle. They will tell you how many days will pass before rain comes.*

The proverb errs in being specific about the number of stars visible and the number of days left before a rain. Otherwise, if there are but a few stars visible, it has merit in its unspoken acknowledgment that rain is near. The moisture-laden atmosphere that is producing the halo is also hiding most of the stars from view.

Though we've mentioned only the moon here, the halo can also be seen encircling the stars and the sun when their light is being reflected off high-altitude ice crystals. When thus seen, they likewise promise rain. The sun halo is much like that of the moon — white with a red border sometimes within it. Other haloes are usually of a reddish tint. The haloed sun prompted this gem of American Indian imagery:

> *When the sun retires to his house, it is going to rain outside.*

To the Netherlanders of centuries ago, the sun's halo was to be more trusted than the moon's, an opinion that they set to rhyme:

> *A ring around the moon*
> *May pass away soon.*
> *But a ring round the sun*
> *Gives water in the tun.*

The halo should not be confused with a similar but quite different phenomenon, the corona. The corona is a small ring of light — reddish along its outer border and bluish within — that appears when the light from any bright object is being reflected through an atmosphere misty with water vapor. Like the halo, though smaller, the corona can encircle the sun, moon, and stars. It, too, carries a message of the coming weather. When it grows larger, it promises approaching fair weather by signaling the evaporation of water droplets in the clouds. A decrease in its size means that the water droplets are on the increase, and rain is in the offing.

The Matter of Shape

Let's turn now to the moon's crescent shape during the periods of waxing and waning. That shape has prompted several weather prophecies. With one exception, all are considered false. The exception limits itself to a possibility:

> *Sharp horns do threaten windy weather.*

At times, when the air is clear, the outline of the crescent moon will have a fuzzy look to it. Accounting for the fuzziness are varying temperatures in the atmosphere. But then comes a night when the tips of the crescent — its "horns" — sharpen and grow more distinct, with the fuzziness decreasing or disappearing altogether. The change is caused by high winds that tend to equalize the varying temperatures by "mixing" them. Since high-altitude winds have the habit of moving downward, there is a strong likelihood that they will soon reach the surface of the earth.

Now the falsehoods:

> *It will not rain when the horns are turned upward because they are holding in the water. Rain comes when the horns are turned downward, for then the water spills out.*

> *The crescent moon holds or spills water for the coming month.*

> *When the moon lies on her back,*
> *She sucks the wet into her lap.*

> *When you can hang your powder horn on the moon, do just that.*

These are all age-old concepts. They were born of the same marvelous but quite mistaken leaps of imagination that conceived of the crescent moon as a vehicle that carried the dead to the hereafter because it resembled a ship. Here, because it looked like a bowl or dipper, the crescent was thought able to hold or release the waters that fell as rain, with all depending on the upward or downward tilt of its horns. It's a clever and imaginative idea, but one that meteorologists say has no meaning.

The powder horn prediction comes from the American Indian. It indicates an upward turn of the crescent; otherwise, the powder horn's shoulder strap would slip off. What the prediction is saying is that you should put away your hunting gear because the ground is going to be too dry for good stalking. Most Indians preferred to hunt when the earth was wet. The tracks left by game were then easier to see.

While we're on the subject of falsehoods, let's turn from predictions to two general comments on the moon's behavior, both of them ancient in origin:

| *The full moon eats the clouds.*

| *The moon grows fat on clouds.*

Both observations are false only in that they are ancient misreadings of an activity in which the moon plays no actual part. They concern the high and somewhat detached clouds that we often see late in the afternoon, especially on a summer day. At dusk, they lose their heat and grow colder, cooling the air around them. The cooler — and, consequently, denser — air sinks earthward, taking the clouds with it. On arriving at a sufficiently low altitude, they encounter warmer air and begin to disappear through evaporation. The disappearance can occur during any lunar phase but is most evident when the moon is near or at its fullness and thus is best able to cast a strong light on the fading clouds as it rises above the horizon. Hence, to the ancients, it was "eating" and "growing fat" on the clouds.

HERSCHEL'S LUNAR CHART

Though the belief that the moon exerts little or no effect on our weather has long been a basic meteorological view, it has not won the heart of every scientist in recent years. Thought to have disagreed with it was the distinguished British astronomer, mathematician, and philosopher Sir John Herschel (1792–1871). He is credited with thinking so much of the moon's influence that he developed a chart that predicted specific weathers based on the moon's phases and the hours of their appearance. Whether Herschel was actually convinced of the moon's influence is a matter of question today because he reportedly later denied authorship of the chart. Whatever the case, the chart itself has been dismissed as meaningless, one of those misguided curiosities that are so often born of splendid minds. Nevertheless, we'll close this chapter with it as a matter of interest and good fun. It may be enjoyable to check it out for yourself — especially if you're an insomniac — to see if it works, at all or on occasion.

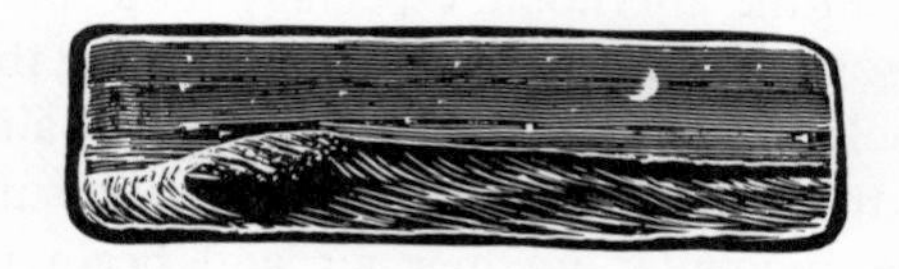

HERSCHEL'S LUNAR CHART

In summer, if the new moon, first-quarter moon, full moon, or last-quarter moon occurs at the times listed in the left-hand column, the weather conditions in the right-hand column will prevail:

12 midnight to 2 A.M.	Fair
2 A.M. to 4 A.M.	Cold and showers
4 A.M. to 6 A.M.	Rain
6 A.M. to 8 A.M.	Wind and rain
8 A.M. to 10 A.M.	Changeable
10 A.M. to 12 noon	Intermittent showers
12 noon to 2 P.M.	Heavy rain
2 P.M. to 4 P.M.	Changeable
4 P.M. to 6 P.M.	Fair
6 P.M. to 8 P.M.	Fair (if wind northwest)
8 P.M. to 10 P.M.	Rain (if wind south or southwest)
10 P.M. to 12 midnight	Fair

In winter, if the new moon, first-quarter moon, full moon, or last-quarter moon occurs at the times below, you may expect:

12 midnight to 2 A.M.	Frost (if wind is not from southwest)
2 A.M. to 4 A.M.	Snow and wind
4 A.M. to 6 A.M.	Rain
6 A.M. to 8 A.M.	Stormy
8 A.M. to 10 A.M.	Cold (if wind west)
10 A.M. to 12 noon	Cold and high winds
12 noon to 2 P.M.	Snow and rain
2 P.M. to 4 P.M.	Fair and mild
4 P.M. to 6 P.M.	Fair
6 P.M. to 8 P.M.	Fair and frosty (if wind north)
8 P.M. to 10 P.M.	Rain and snow (if wind south)
10 P.M. to 12 midnight	Fair and frosty

CHAPTER FOUR

The Restless Sky: The Wind

Lo, as the wind is, so is mortal life,
A moan, a sigh, a sob, a storm, a strife.

— EDWIN ARNOLD (1832–1904)
From: "The Deva's Song"

THIS CHAPTER begins with a point made earlier about the sun. Because of the earth's tilt, its equatorial band receives the greatest share of sunlight throughout the course of any year. The air there is heated greatly and, rendered less dense by the warming, rises to move away toward the northern and southern polar regions. En route some of the air is deflected back to the equator, for reasons that we'll see later. The remainder, cooling as it travels, makes its way to the polar regions, where it becomes so dense and heavy that it sinks to the earth. From there, it works its way back to the equator. On arriving home, it fills the void left by air presently being heated and is itself warmed and readied for another outbound passage. This perpetual departure from and return to the equatorial band is felt as the ever-changing force that British poet Edwin Arnold so ably compared to human life: the wind.

In its many moods, the wind has been recognized, respected, and feared since the beginning of time as a major weather maker — the bringer of fair and dark skies, the invisible breath that, on the one hand, can cool and calm when it comes gently from the sea of a summer afternoon but, on the other, can chill to the bone when it ices over, or terrify and kill when, in a witless rage, it conjures up the tornado's funnel cloud.

AS THE ANCIENTS FELT IT

It is little wonder, then, that the ancients bowed to the wind as a sacred power. The story here is much the same as those of the sun and moon. It begins with the early peoples who thought of the wind as a minor deity. To some, it was a messenger of the gods, the carrier of news that could be good or bad depending on the direction from which it arrived — in part, a form of early weathercasting. A north wind, for example, signaled intense cold or, by a simple leap of the imagination, an unhappy event. Around the Mediterranean, a harsh northeaster marked the approach of dry weather and was easily translated into an announcement of drought, death, and pestilence.

To the Pueblo Indians of the American Southwest, it was a god that took several forms. Two were said to be an old woman and an old man. The woman lived in a cave at the center of the world; people suffering rheumatism could appeal for relief by offering her grain, turkey feathers, and pollen. The old man was thought to have died; otherwise, so the Indians believed, the local winds would assuredly have been worse than they actually were. Another was a "sickness god" who lurked near dwelling places and brought disease and pestilence.

The idea that sickness was carried by some god or imp who crouched in hiding near or about houses was widespread in the ancient world. In one of its earliest forms, it was to be found among the Sumerians of that cradle of civilization, Mesopotamia. Doors and windows were kept shut so that the creature could not leap through with his evil gift. It is a concept that remains in our language today. We are speaking as the ancients did when we talk of "catching" a cold.

Several peoples, among them the Egyptians and Greeks, looked on the wind as a collection of major gods. Each deity in the group represented a major direction from whence the wind came and was endowed with characteristics consistent with those of its wind. For example, the Greek god of the north wind was Boreas, a warmly clothed old man who spent his time blowing through a conch shell. The god of the east wind — for the Greeks a warm wind — was Eurus (or Argestes or Apeliotes), a scantily clad young man.

These are but a handful of the characterizations given the wind gods by the ancients. In a veritable hodge-podge of depictions, those gods, whether of major or minor rank, were variously seen as capricious, gentle, mean, fast-growing, and suddenly dying creatures, all of them capable of an unrestrained power if they were of a mind to use it. In one especially vigorous flight of fancy, they were described by some people as gods with their feet pointing backward so that they could move faster. They were also widely envisioned as musicians, with Pan a chief figure among this number; their favorite instruments seem to have been the reed pipe and the harp. And, of course, because of their ability to create their familiar sound when swirling about a house, they were viewed as singers and whistlers. This supposed latter talent may be behind an old superstition that lingers to this day in Europe and the United States. The idea may be that one whistler is sure to attract another:

| *Whistle when you want the wind to blow.*

Recognizing both its unrestrained power and its similarity to the human breath, a number of cultures believed the wind to be the force that brought life, while others saw it as an evil thing meant to take away life and gave it such names as the "death demon" or the "snatcher of souls." The Egyptians and Greeks were among those who sensed evil in it.

THE FOLKLORE OF THE WIND

Down through the ages, the concept of the wind as a force of good and bad — one, the other, or both — has been the subject of some interesting and, on occasion, entertaining folk sayings, beliefs, and tales. Beginning with a pair still cherished in Ireland, here are some of the most time-honored sayings:

Three best friends and three worst enemies: fire, wind, and rain.

Three enemies of the body: wind, smoke, and fleas.

The Devil never sent the wind,
But he would sail with it.

— ENGLAND

Hoist your sails when the wind is fair.

— ENGLAND

The Devil is busy in a high wind.

And these blunt, down-to-earth wisdoms, the first two from Ireland and the last from an England yet to embrace the rhetorical proprieties of the Victorian era:

A windy day is not the day for thatching.

He may die of wind but he'll never die of wisdom.

Piss not against the wind.

As for folk beliefs: in a variation of the age-old "Tuesday's child" rhyme, a number of peoples once held — and some are still charmed by the idea — that you were fated to lead a certain life in keeping with the wind direction at the time of your birth. Were you lucky enough to be born when the wind was from the east, you would garner riches and never know want. Were it from the south, you would enjoy interesting friends. However, were it from the north, you were destined for a lifetime of war. And, were it from the west, you would receive only the barest of life's necessities.

And what if there were no wind at all? Yours was to be the life of a fool.

Some of the wind's best folk tales come from the American Indians and have to do with bringing its force under control. In the eastern regions of our continent, the hero of a widely told story is the spirit who attacks the great bird responsible for the wind and breaks its wing; on healing, the wing is smaller and able to produce only gentle winds when the bird again takes flight.

From the Northwest comes the myth of the young spirit who corners the wind god and threatens to shoot an arrow into him, only to relent when his prisoner vows not to blow constantly as has been his habit.

THE WINDS: THE FACTS OF THE MATTER

Meteorology has shown us that the wind is born of the intense solar heating along the equatorial band. This heating and the movement it causes, however, are only part of the story. Playing a role also in the manufacture of our winds is the earth's rotation on its axis, a rotation that results in one complete revolution every 24 hours. Were our planet hanging motionless in space, we would still have the wind, but it would be vastly different. Heated at the equator, it would rise as it does now, move northward and southward at high altitudes, and, on entering the polar regions, grow heavy with the cold and sink to the surface. From there, it would venture back to the equator. At ground level here in the northern hemisphere, we would feel this southward movement as the wind. It would be a wind of a constant speed.

But, with the earth completing one full spin on its axis every 24 hours, we are living on anything but a motionless planet. A simple equation shows just how much in motion things really are. Since the earth's circumference at the equator measures 25,000 miles and since the spin is in an eastward direction, this means that, were you this moment standing at any point along the equator, you would be traveling eastward at a speed of just under 1,000 miles an hour. That speed not only interferes with a smooth-flowing air movement away from and back to the equator, but it also deflects the movement into a general pattern that sends the earth's winds flowing in various directions.

In addition, since our planet is a spheroid, the speed of its rotation steadily decreases as its surface falls away to the north and south of the equator. Should you shift your position to some point along 10° North Latitude, you'd be traveling at 985 miles an hour. At 40° N., you'd be down to 770 mph; at 80° N., 175 mph; and at the North Pole — 90° N. — you'd be standing dead still. These differing speeds (which are matched, of course, in the southern hemisphere) affect the flow and behavior of the winds as they are sent through their general pattern. That general pattern divides the world into seven latitudinal wind bands, or belts. The first, the equatorial band, extends into both the northern and southern hemispheres. Then each hemisphere contains three additional bands. Each band affects the air flow in a distinct way and forms it into a wind system.

Latitudinal Bands and Wind Systems

As the heated air in the equatorial belt rises and embarks for the polar regions, the earth's rotation sends it along a curving path. In our northern hemisphere, the air is first deflected eastward. By the time the invisible mass nears 30° N. Latitude, however, it has

THE EARTH'S WIND SYSTEMS. *Banding the equator is the system known as the doldrums. Next, to the north and south of the doldrums, are the trade-winds bands. Then, still farther north and south, are the bands predominated by the prevailing westerlies. Finally, at the top and bottom of the world, are the polar-winds bands.*

cooled considerably, and heavier again, much of it sinks to lower altitudes and begins a return to the equator, making a westward turn to come about to its homeward course. Consequently, the winds in the band between the equatorial belt and 30° N. flow from the northeast, forming the system known as the trade winds, so called because, in the long-ago days of sailing vessels, their direction facilitated the passage of merchant ships westward bound from Europe to the New World and the Orient.

Not all the cooling air is sent southward by the time 30° N. is attained. Some is flung northward and passes through a second band, which lies between 30° and 60° N. Here, the flow is turned so that winds travel from west to east — or, specifically, along an oblique course that, depending much on the season of the year, can run from slightly south of west to slightly north of west — and form the system known as the prevailing westerlies. (All wind directions are designated by the direction *from* which they flow, with north winds coming from the north, southwest coming from the southwest, and so on.)

Another point of deflection shows itself at about 60° N. The winds enter a third band and shift for a final time, turning so that they flow from the northeast. Now heavy with the cold — and called the polar easterlies — they sink to the surface and begin the return journey to the equator.

The same bands are seen in the same latitudes south of the equator. The system in each of the southern hemisphere's bands is the same as ours, but because that flow is along the lower half of a sphere, its direction of origin is reversed: the southern trades flow toward the equator from the southeast; the prevailing westerlies come from a point slightly north of west; and the polar easterlies rise from the southeast.

Wind Systems and Climate

Each of the latitudinal bands has its own distinctive climatic conditions. The heated, rising air along the equatorial band, for instance, means little or no wind at the surface. The region is commonly marked by the condition known as the doldrums — prolonged stretches of deadly calm weather that, capable of stalling a ship under sail for days or weeks on end while its water and food supplies dwindled away, were dreaded by seamen of earlier times. Additionally, the band's heated air is thick with moisture and can bring heavy rains and, if conditions are right, hurricanes and typhoons.

The trade-winds band is marked by steady winds, with the skies near its northern edge being customarily clear, while farther south, there are often thick clouds and rainfall that can range from the showery to the heavy. The rains are triggered when the cooling and southward-moving trades clash with the heated air rising above the doldrums.

Within the band is a stretch known as the horse latitudes, which are characterized by a weak and sometimes completely dead wind. They come by their name because Spanish galleons bound for the New World with horses aboard were often becalmed and ran out of fodder and water for the animals while trying to make their way through the area. The crews then threw the starving creatures overboard. Records of the time say that the sea was, on occasion, littered with the bodies of dead and dying horses.

The prevailing westerlies are in play above all of the United States except Florida and the coasts along the Gulf of Mexico. Except for several conditions, the nation's weather would be very stable because of the slow cooling of the winds as they moved north and east. Alternating would be stretches of fair and rainy skies. As things are, our weather is subject to major changes, some of them violent, because of such conditions as the passage of the air over various land contours (from low deserts to towering mountains); the clash of the westerlies with the much colder air masses moving southward from the North Pole; and the turbulent meeting with the warmer trades coming up from the South.

THE WIND AND WEATHER LORE

The pattern of flow away from and back to the equator gives us a general picture of the various directions taken by the winds, along with some idea of the climates to be found in the latitudinal band. But it cannot tell us much about the many different weathers to be found within the bands. Those weathers are shaped by the actions of various factors on the winds, and by the actions of the winds on various factors. Such conditions as the three mentioned above in connection with our U.S. winds come into play, as do, for example, the temperature differences between land and sea winds, and the changes in atmospheric pressure caused by the heating and cooling of the moving air.

For the countless observers who have given us the literature of weather lore, one of the most important of these factors is the rise and fall in atmospheric pressure that accompanies the heating and cooling of the moving air. The literature abounds with weather-to-come predictions based on wind direction. Largely responsible for them is that rise and fall.

High and Low Pressure Systems

So that the predictions will make sense, we need to talk briefly about high and low pressure systems. As you will recall from Chapter One, our atmosphere is at its most dense at the earth's surface, exerting a pressure there of 14.7 pounds per square inch. As the air at the surface warms, its density is reduced; it expands, lightens, and rises, reducing the pressure at the surface accordingly. Conversely, when cold, its density thickens, causing it to sink earthward and increase the pressure there.

High pressure systems (made up of cooler, denser air) and low pressure systems (consisting of warm, less dense air) take shape as the winds move across the globe. They can confine themselves to local areas or can spread across vast expanses. In general, a high

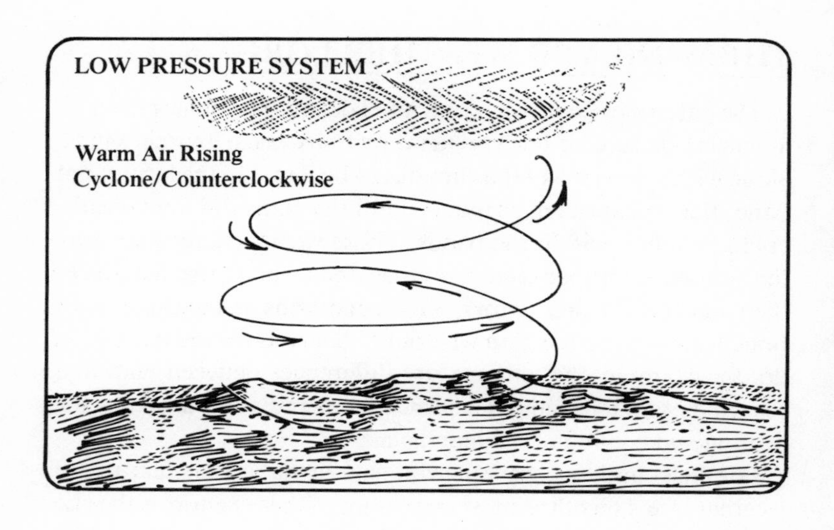

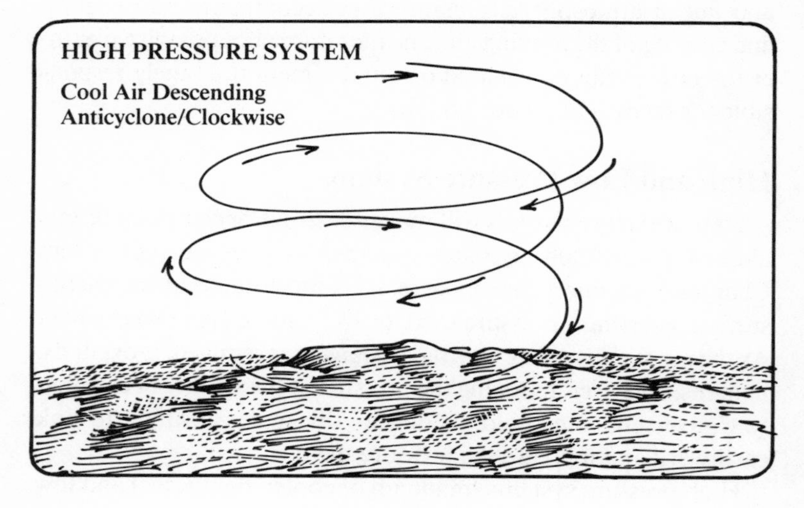

SPIRALING WIND PATTERNS *that are created by high pressure (bottom) and low pressure (top) systems.*

pressure system produces fair weather. Its low pressure counterpart brings cloudiness, a drop in barometric pressure, and a rise in humidity — all of them conditions that, though often ending in heavy cloudiness, are the hallmarks of approaching rain or snow.

High and low pressure systems each generate winds from a certain direction. Those winds are most strongly felt at and near ground level, with their influence diminishing through the higher altitudes where the air is thinner and, as a result, the pressure less.

In the northern hemisphere, when cool air descends to the surface to form a high pressure system, it creates a spiraling wind pattern that turns in a clockwise fashion (the pattern is reversed in the southern hemisphere). That spiral is called by several names but is best known simply as a "high." High pressure systems customarily bring fair weather. In our latitudes, though high and low pressure systems can induce winds from various directions, fair weather is usually accompanied by winds from some point in the west.

But, when warm air rises and threatens us with bad weather, it is marked by a spiraling pattern that turns in a counterclockwise direction (again, the pattern is reversed in the southern hemisphere). In common with the high pressure system, it has several names but is most often referred to as a "low." In many areas within our latitudinal zone, bad weather is announced by winds that shift and then strike us from some point in the east.

And so it is that the wind directions created by the spirals are the keys to many of the forecasts found in weather lore. Because we live within the band of the prevailing westerlies, the weather in most of the United States (and much of Europe) is carried to us on a west wind and flows to the east. A high, then, tells us that the weather coming our way is to be fair. The low's spiral, bringing a wind from some point in the east, warns of troublesome skies ahead.

The direction of the wind has long played a part not only in weather lore but also in formal meteorological forecasting. The

United States Department of Agriculture in its early years thought so much of the wind's predictive abilities that it issued the following guidelines for farmers. They can serve us well as general guides to what the direction of the wind signifies for the immediate future.

> *Westerly winds are fair-weather winds.*

> *When the wind shifts from east to west during a storm, clearing follows.*

> *Easterly winds bring rain. Northeast winds in winter bring heavy snow.*

The USDA rules gave the official stamp of approval to one of weather lore's most venerable and valid proverbs:

> *Every wind has its weather.*

— SIR FRANCIS BACON (1561–1626)

And now let's look at the weather lore that surrounds wind direction. We'll begin with that in our latitudes — the west wind.

The West Wind

Among the best known of the west-wind proverbs to come down through the centuries are the following four. The first three, so similar in wording, were undoubtedly borrowed from each other; which of them provided the original thought is anybody's guess.

> *But when the wind is in the west,*
> *There it is the very best.*

— IZAAK WALTON (1593–1683)
From: *The Compleat Angler*

> *When the wind is in the west,*
> *The weather is at its best.*

> *The wind in the west*
> *Suits everyone the best.*

> *A west wind is a favorable wind.*

These apply to much of our latitudinal band but do not hold true everywhere within it. Although they will prove sound wherever the west wind is dry because it is blowing across interior land surfaces, they are not to be trusted in spots where the wind is arriving from the sea. Two such examples in the United States are along the Gulf Coast of Florida and stretches of the Pacific Coast. In these and similar areas, the following words apply:

> *When ye see a cloud rise out of the west, straightway ye say, there cometh a shower; and so it is.*
>
> — LUKE 12:54

Still, as a general rule of thumb in our latitudinal band, the west wind prophecies will stand us in good stead:

> *Do business with men when the wind is in the northwest when the barometer is high.*
>
> — BENJAMIN FRANKLIN (1706–1790)

> *A west wind like an honest man goes to bed*
> *at sundown.*

Franklin's observation is based on the idea that we humans are made more congenial, active, and alert by dry, invigorating weather and, consequently, bring to our business dealings a better and more cooperative mood. As for the west wind going to bed at sundown, the proverb stems from the fact that the force of the wind is customarily lessened by the cooling of the land after the sun has set.

The East Wind

While virtually all the west-wind proverbs are on the happy side, matters immediately reverse themselves with the arrival of the low pressure spiral that turns the wind and brings it from some point in the east. Now come the conditions that characterize an arriving storm — increasing cloudiness, a drop in barometric pressure, and a rise in humidity.

> *When the wind is in the east,*
> *'Tis neither good for man nor beast.*
>
> — Izaak Walton
> From: *The Compleat Angler*

> *Wind from the east*
> *Is good for neither man nor beast.*
>
> — Ireland

> *The wind from the northeast,*
> *Neither good for man nor beast.*

> *Winds from the northeast*
> *Bring storms of ice fruit* [hail].
>
> — Zuni Indians

Then:

> *An easterly wind is like a boring guest that hasn't sense enough to leave.*

This last saying applies mainly to coastal areas with the ocean to the east. There, the storm with an easterly wind has shown the habit of hanging about for 2 or 3 days. Often, during the course of the storm, the wind direction shifts back and forth between east and northeast.

> *When the smoke goes west,*
> *Gude weather is past.*
> *When the smoke goes east,*
> *Gude weather comes neist.*
>
> — ENGLAND

If you're without a weather vane on your roof, one of the best indicators of wind direction is, obviously, the path along which smoke is blown. At heart, the proverb above is speaking of the wind shift that, at some point in a storm, sees the wind again shift west and, blowing the smoke eastward, promises the return of fair weather.

> *A veering wind, fair weather.*
> *A backing wind, foul weather.*

> *A veering wind will clear the sky.*
> *A backing wind says storms are nigh.*

These two proverbs are thought to have been the invention of the always watchful mariners of old. As we do today, they defined a veering wind in the northern hemisphere as one that turns in the direction taken by the spiral when a high is at hand. A backing wind turns counterclockwise, indicating the formation of a low with its promise of bad weather to come.

Related to the two proverbs is this New England observation:

> *When you see a whirlwind, you know it's going*
> *to rain.*

The saying is partially true. It will work only if the whirlwind is turning counterclockwise and giving away the fact that it's being generated by a low pressure system.

Here are two more interesting proverbs. The first comes from the England of centuries ago; the second from the United States, perhaps dating back to colonial times:

> *Easterly wind and rain,*
> *Bring cockles here from Spain.*

> *A cow with its tail to the west*
> *Makes weather the best.*
> *A cow with its tail to the east*
> *Makes weather the least.*

"Cockles," thought by British farmers of old to have originated in Spain, is a disease that results when a type of parasite attacks wheat and turns it black. The name itself refers to an excrescence that forms on the wheat and resembles the seed of the corn cockle plant.

And the cow with its weather vane tail: All sensible animals graze with their backs to the wind so that they are able to detect the scent of enemies approaching from the rear. When they turn their tails eastward, they're not only protecting themselves but also warning us that bad weather is on the way.

> *The east wind brings aches and pains.*

As we'll see in greater detail in Chapter Six, the increasing easterly wind, the fall in barometric pressure, and the rise in humidity that routinely precede a storm can have some pretty uncomfortable effects on such human problems as aging muscles and joints, surgical scars, and old broken bones. The Irish long ago expressed it this way:

> *The word goes to the wind but the blow goes*
> *to the bone.*

While its prophecies depict it as a villain, the east wind is not disliked in all parts of the world. It is highly regarded in those parched areas that welcome the rain it brings. And, in some spots, it signals the arrival of fair weather. Perhaps the views in these regions account for the earlier-mentioned superstition about wind direction at the time of birth: that the child who comes into the world with an east wind is due to enjoy a lifetime of riches, while the west-wind child will receive only life's barest necessities.

North and South Winds

Though most of the United States lies within the band of the prevailing westerlies, the continent is also subject to great air masses moving in from points in the north and south. The former consist of cold air moving southward back to the equator from the polar regions, while the latter are made up of warm tropical air. When they encounter the prevailing westerlies (or each other), the collision can trigger such weather upheavals as rain, gales, snow, hail, thunderstorms, and, if the angle of collision is just right, tornadoes. And so the following proverbs have made their way into the literature of weather lore:

> *The north wind doth blow*
> *And we shall have snow.*

> *When the wind is in the south,*
> *It's in the rain's mouth.*

The north wind prophecy is heard mainly in the northern regions of Europe and throughout much of the United States. The areas along the Mediterranean, because of the continental mass to their north, have found the north wind to be the forerunner of dry weather. Behind the south wind forecast is the fact that the counterclockwise turn created by a low brings the wind from that direction as well as from the east.

Finally, we come to Britain's King Alfred (circa 848–899) who not only defeated the invading Danes but also took time to write about the weather. In his collection of verse, *Poems,* he attempted to encompass, in three brief stanzas, all that we need to know of wind directions and what they foretell:

> *When the wind southwest*
> *Under the cloud blows low,*
> *Field flowers wax their best,*
> *Fain to be glad and grow.*
>
> *But when east and by north*
> *The stark storm strongly blows,*
> *Speedily he drives forth*
> *All beauty from the rose.*
>
> *So with a stern needs-be*
> *The northern blast doth dash*
> *And beat the wide waste sea,*
> *That it the land may lash.*

Along with King Alfred, we may talk all we wish about wind direction and the weather it promises, but the Spanish must have the final say here. In just eight words they have come up with the ultimate truth:

> *When God wills, it rains with any wind.*

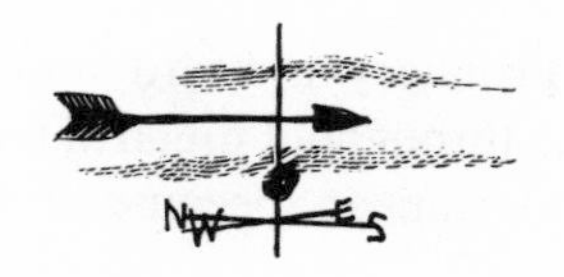

General Prophecies

> *No weather is ill*
> *When the winds are still.*

We turn now to the predictions and truths in which, like the above proverb, the direction of the wind is not mentioned. Other factors take center stage. We begin with:

> *Rain long foretold, long last.*
> *Short notice, soon past.*

The proverb is based on the behavior of what are called weather fronts. When masses of cold and warm air meet, the point of their encounter is known as a front. Like its military forebear, the weather front is the scene of conflict as one wind-driven air mass tries to overcome the other. The battle usually results in bad weather.

There are several types of weather fronts. For our purposes, it is necessary to mention just two — the warm front and the cold front. The former occurs when a mass of warm air advances on a mass of cold air and successfully replaces it. The latter, obviously, occurs when a mass of cold air works its way beneath a mass of warm. The widths of both can stretch for several hundred miles.

The two fronts behave in different ways and, in so doing, give us the proverb. The line "Rain long foretold, long last" speaks of the warm front's habit of passing lazily overhead (its speed averages about 15 mph, but can be slower on occasion) and allowing several hours, usually about ten, to elapse before releasing its rain. When the rain does come, it hangs about for a day or so. The cold front, on the other hand, moves in quickly (at an average of 20 mph, but customarily faster in winter), bringing a storm that, while routinely harsher than the warm front's and sometimes even violent, remains but a short while, usually no more than a few hours. Hence, the final line, "Short notice, soon past."

> *High altitude winds soon descend to earth.*

This saying has merit. Winds do tend to occur at higher altitudes and then, over a period of hours, settle to earth.

> *The whispering grove*
> *Tells of a storm to come.*

A rising wind, of course, is one of the characteristic signs of approaching bad weather. Hence, when the grove — whether it be a forest or a stand of trees on your property — begins to "whisper" as the wind flows through it, you can look for a storm.

> *The sharper the blast,*
> *The sooner it's past.*

> *The worst winds come at the end of a storm.*

Just as it can suggest the approach of a storm, so can the wind's intensity indicate its imminent departure. Quite correctly, weather lorists long ago noted the wind's habit of increasing in the final hours of a storm and, by its very force, indicating that its energy would soon be spent.

> *The winds of the daytime wrestle and fight*
> *Longer and stronger than those of the night.*

This proverb applies to the land only. Behind it is the fact that moving air at or near ground level is more greatly mixed with the upper air during the day than at night. This increased "mixing," of course, is because the sunlight quickly heats surface air and causes it to rise and meet the higher-altitude air. As the land air rapidly cools at night, the process is retarded. Should a land wind remain strong at night, it is a good indication of bad weather to come. The proverb does not apply to the sea because the night air there cools more slowly and thus allows the winds to maintain their strength.

> *When the glass falls low,*
> *Prepare for a blow.*
> *When it rises high,*
> *Let all your kites fly.*

> *When the wind backs and the weather glass falls,*
> *Then be on your guard against gales and squalls.*

The "glass" is the barometer, the instrument that measures air pressure. When the mercury level in the barometer falls, a low is at hand and anything from unsettled weather to those "gales and squalls" is in the offing.

The fact is that the barometer never falls significantly in atmospheric conditions other than those connected with a storm. Nor does it ever rise appreciably except in conditions associated with fair weather.

MEASURING THE WIND

In 1805, Britain's Admiral Sir Francis Beaufort (1774–1857) devised a scale to estimate wind speeds and their effects on sailing ships. With each wind velocity given a number somewhere between 0 and 12, the Beaufort Scale is still used today to measure wind strengths at sea and also has come to serve as a measure for determining the effects of land winds of various speeds. The Scale, which is printed here as a matter of interest for readers not acquainted with it, gives velocity in miles per hour and knots,

THE BEAUFORT WIND SCALE

NO.	MPH	KNOTS	DESCRIPTION	VISUAL CLUE
0	0-1	0-1	Calm	Smoke rises vertically
1	1-3	1-3	Light air	Smoke drifts slowly
2	4-7	4-6	Slight breeze	Leaves rustle
3	8-12	7-10	Gentle breeze	Leaves and twigs in motion
4	13-18	11-16	Moderate breeze	Small branches move
5	19-24	17-21	Fresh breeze	Small trees sway
6	25-31	22-27	Strong breeze	Large branches sway
7	32-38	28-33	Moderate gale	Whole trees in motion
8	39-46	34-40	Fresh gale	Twigs break off trees
9	47-54	41-47	Strong gale	Branches break
10	55-63	48-55	Whole gale	Trees break and blow down
11	64-72	56-63	Storm	Widespread damage
12	73-83	64-71	Hurricane	Extreme damage

describes ascending wind strengths, and provides visual clues for identifying each strength.

* * *

We turn next to the clouds — in all their beauty, sometimes gossamer thin, sometimes thick and comforting, and sometimes bleak and darkly foreboding — and what they tell us of the weather to come.

CHAPTER FIVE

Sculptures in the Sky: The Clouds

Slowly climb the moon-touched mountains
Up their stairway to the sky,
Slowly each cloud ascending,
Seems a soul that passed on high.

— SAMUEL M. HAGERMAN (1848–1905)
From: "Silence"

SINCE THE DAWN of time, in their myriad shapes and majestic windborne passages across the heavens, the clouds have drawn the human eye skyward and have inspired some of poetry's most imaginative lines and some of the mind's most unusual thinking. From the lofty to the lowering, and from the summery soft and gentle to the wintry dark and foreboding, their beauty — a beauty of contrasts — has moved the poet to compare their moods with life, death, and love. Those same contrasts long ago prompted the mind to develop two diametrically opposed views of the clouds.

On the one hand, in their loftiness and gentleness, the ancient mind saw them as variously representing sanctity, wisdom, protection, good fortune, and high ambition. The belief that they were protectors sprang from a very practical observation in regions of blazing heat. There, a passing cloud often provided the only relief from a sun that sought to wither all life. As for good fortune and high ambition, these ideas had to do with an upward reaching of the human spirit. In China, for instance, the sight of a young boy flying a kite toward the clouds meant that he would soon reach his goals in life.

But, on the other hand, because clouds are capable of a somber and restless darkness, they were early associated with dreariness, ignorance, mystery, and trouble. And, because the eye can neither penetrate nor see through their folds and mists, they represented short-sightedness. For the same reason, they were thought of as obscuring the great truths that could be man's if only he had the vision to see them.

Joining these contrasting views was the belief that, like the sun and moon and other natural phenomena, the clouds were sacred beings. For some peoples, they were the armies of the gods, passing in majestic review when the sky was quiet, engaging in battle when the sky boiled with a storm. The Old Testament spoke of them as being the dust of Jehovah's feet. To the early Christian, they represented God's presence. In several cultures, they were seen as the breath of the gods.

Additionally, the ancient imagination conceived them to be the celestial equivalents of earthbound beings. For some people, they were divine ships at sail on an endless sea of blue. For others, they were gigantic cattle, sheep, and horses grazing or cavorting overhead. When they were seen moving in different directions at different altitudes (a commonplace occurrence caused by conflicting air currents), the ancients said that some of the animals were running backward.

Because they so often heralded an approaching rain, the clouds were viewed widely as messengers. Since the rain could be either life-giving or life-taking, the messages could portend a coming of good or evil. We reveal our continuing emotional ties with our earliest forebears whenever we fall back on two of the western world's most venerable clichés:

| *Every cloud has a silver lining.*

| *To be under a cloud.*

Both sayings, with the one so optimistic and the other speaking of a life suffering humiliation or suspicion, can be traced back several hundred years. One of the earliest expressions of the first comes from the pen of John Milton (1608–1674) and is to be found in his narrative poem, *Comus:*

> *Was I deceived or did a sable cloud*
> *Turn forth her silver lining on the night?*

Since then, the saying, in forms more familiar to us, has found its way into the works of Mark Twain, Louisa May Alcott, Gilbert and Sullivan, showman P. T. Barnum, and mystery writer Mignon G. Eberhart.

The ancient view of the clouds was complex, as are the clouds themselves in their various formations and their effects on our emotions. But, no matter what they can do to our feelings in their glory on a summer's day or their sullenness as they carry a winter storm to us, these "sculptures in the sky" are the products of a simple and easily explained process.

CLOUDS IN THE MAKING

Clouds are sculpted when a quantity of air is cooled to or below its dew point — that point at which its water vapor begins to condense and become visible. On condensing, the vapor takes the shape of tiny water droplets or, if the surrounding atmosphere is cold enough, ice crystals. Clinging to specks of dust, infinitesimal bits of airborne minerals, and traces of salt from the sea, the droplets and crystals mold themselves into clouds of various types. The droplets do not fall as rain because they are too small and weightless for gravity to pull them earthward. Until the actions within the cloud cause them to balloon to an appropriate size, they will do nothing but ride on the surrounding air currents.

Because the clouds are carriers of moisture and because they are always on the scene when it rains or snows, many of us principally think of them in connection with stormy weather. But, as one of the oldest and possibly the most obvious of all folk proverbs puts it, such is not the case at all:

> *All clouds bring not rain.*

Indeed they don't; some promise agreeable skies, and others threaten anything from unsettled weather to the severest of storms. The promise and the threat are to be seen in the shape, the texture, the tint, the movement, and the interplay one with the other of the various cloud types. All these factors combine to make the clouds one of the best natural forecasters we have. As a result, every weather watcher — from the simply curious observer to the worried farmer and seaman or the amateur and professional meteorologist — has looked to them for clues of how the skies plan to behave in the next hours or days.

To understand the many clues at hand, we need to learn something of the various cloud types. For our purposes, we will focus on only two general types — heaped and layered — into which all cloud classes and species can be placed. Each of the two fashions its clouds in its own specific way. Once formed, the clouds within each type can suggest certain weather trends.

THE HEAPED CLOUD

> *If woolly fleeces spread the heavenly way,*
> *Be sure no rain disturbs the summer's day.*

> *When white clouds cover the heavenly way,*
> *No rain will mar your plans that day.*

If on the ocean's bosom clouds appear,
While the blue vault above is bright and clear,
These signs by shepherds and by sailors seen,
Give pleasing hope of days and nights serene.

— ARATUS

These three forecasts refer to a member of the cumulus (meaning accumulated) family — the group that makes up the heaped category. The family members are among the most distinctive and easily recognized of all clouds. To identify any cumulus cloud, simply recall the various descriptions that skywatchers have given the family down through the years. Find a cloud that is "piled-up," "cottony," "woolpacklike," "puffy," or "cauliflowerlike," and you've located a cumulus.

The cumulus is the product of unstable air. Specifically, it is formed when a section of the earth's surface radiates heat into the adjacent atmosphere and creates a pocket of warm, moist air. At its base, the pocket is anchored to the ground, but its upper area, lighter than the cool air above it, moves steadily into the sky, simultaneously spreading out in all directions. As it rises, it cools, eventually dropping to or below its dew point and producing the cumulus cloud.

The cumulus usually has a flattish bottom side, which indicates the altitude at which its water vapor is condensing. Its top, fluffy and "piled up" by the rising pocket of warm air, shows the altitudes to which the pocket is ascending.

And what of the three predictions? They are the safest of forecasts if for no other reason than that they refer to a cumulus type — the cumulus humilis — most commonly on view in the summer. True to its name, it is made up of gentle-looking clouds that are puffy, relatively small, widely separated, and longer than they are tall. Additionally, though commonly marked with gray along their undersides (a reflection of the earth's colors), they are colored a whipped-cream white. Their color, along with their puffy "woolly fleece" look, indicates continuing fair weather. Lacking

A CUMULUS CLOUD *takes shape when a section of the earth's surface radiates heat into the adjacent atmosphere and creates a pocket of warm air whose upper area moves steadily into the sky, spreading out in all directions as it travels. As it rises, the pocket cools and, on dropping to or below its dew point, produces the cumulus cloud.*

is that familiar combination of thickness and darkness that promises rain.

Then there is the matter of their smallness and separateness, which enabled Aratus to see that "blue vault above." Small and floating along as distinct individuals, they leave no doubt that, while they themselves are the products of rising, unstable air, the surrounding atmosphere is stable and contains not enough moisture to induce a rain. Finally, though puffing upward, they are long rather than tall; in more formal terms, they are shaped more horizontally than vertically. As long as their development remains on the horizontal, you needn't worry about rain.

Rain becomes a threat when the rising pocket of warm, moist air is of sufficient strength and size to drive the cumulus into a sharp vertical development. Out of that development come our next examples of folk wisdom, all of them sound forecasts:

> *When clouds rise in terraces of white, soon will the country of the corn priests be pierced with arrows of rain.*
>
> — ZUNI INDIANS

> *When the clouds appear like rocks and towers,*
> *The earth's refreshed by frequent showers.*

> *As it happened in the beginning,*
> *As it is happening now,*
> *The sky is covered with high piled clouds;*
> *The earth is covered with misty fog;*
> *The earth is covered with great rains;*
> *And the thunder drums are being heard*
> *In all the four directions of the earth.*
>
> — APACHE INDIANS

As the cumulus is driven into a vertical development, the increasing condensation within its folds causes it to take on a thickening, ballooning, and "rocky" look. During this initial phase of shaping, it is known as cumulus congestus. Then, as the warm air pushes the cloud ever higher and thickens it still further with that ever-increasing condensation, it is called cumulonimbus (nimbus means rain; the term is also used to denote a cloud capable of producing snow). Rain is imminent because, in part through colliding with each other, the water droplets within the cloud blend together, grow in size, and approach the moment when they will be heavy enough for gravity to pull them earthward as rain.

The developing cumulonimbus is a beautiful sight to behold: it is simultaneously massive and graceful. But within its folds all is violent action. There are updrafts created by the rising air, and downdrafts triggered by the rising warm air colliding with the colder upper-altitude air. Over a period of time, the cumulonimbus can build itself to great heights, while its base remains near ground level. In its most impressive form, it becomes the thunderhead, which can reach altitudes between 60,000 and 75,000 feet — and even above. The thunderhead is so named because it commonly produces the electrical storm. When beset by especially violent updrafts and downdrafts, it generates the tornado. The thunderhead is easily recognized not only by its height but also by its distinctive "anvil" crest. This feature is born when high altitude winds catch the uppermost folds of the cloud and carry them along a horizontal path, flattening them and giving them the look of a blacksmith's anvil.

The cumulonimbus is the subject of yet another time-honored axiom:

> *In the morning mountains,*
> *In the evening fountains.*

The proverb is one of the most logical entries to be found in weather lore. When the cumulonimbus takes shape in the forenoon, the greatest heat of the day is yet to come. The rising warm air will continue to thicken the cloud with moisture for hours to come, making the possibility of rain sometime in the late afternoon or early evening more than a good bet.

Cumulus clouds can develop at almost any altitude. With the exception of the cumulonimbus, they change their names from one altitude to another. Near the ground (with their bases generally 6,500 feet above the earth and lower), they are classed as low clouds by meteorologists and are called simply by the family name, cumulus. At heights from 6,000 to 20,000 feet, they are classed as middle clouds; they add "alto" (meaning middle to high) to their name and become altocumulus clouds. At 20,000 feet and above, the classification changes to high clouds and the family name to cirrocumulus. Cirro comes from the term "cirrus" (meaning tendril or curl). In keeping with the name, the cirrocumulus, though still somewhat heaped, is thin and patchy. It often forms a wave pattern high in the sky.

THE LAYERED CLOUD

The layered cloud is divided into two families — the stratus and the cirrus.

The Stratus Family

In appearance, stratus clouds are the exact opposites of the cumulus. Though at certain altitudes they can be fibrous and veil-like, they are customarily described as being sheetlike and featureless.

The manner in which they are formed is responsible for their appearance. Unlike the cumulus, they are not shaped by a rising pocket of warm air. Rather, they appear when a layer of warm air moves into a cool area and is cooled to or below its dew point.

Near the ground, the stratus cloud usually resembles a sheet of fog and is indeed fog at times; on occasion, it is seen in ragged patches, again resembling fog. Tinted from light to dark gray, the stratus often gives the sky a leaden look that seems to threaten rain. However, only a fine drizzle, a light rain, or a light snow usually falls from the stratus because it has little or none of the vertical movement necessary for heavier precipitation. Light though the stratus precipitation is, it can last for several days.

One kind of stratus — the nimbostratus — is a true rain cloud. It ranges in color from light to dark gray and is often accompanied by ragged companions, called scuds, running below it. Like the stratus, its fall of rain or snow can last for an extended period of time.

In common with the cumulus and in an identical manner, the stratus changes its name and classification from one altitude level to another:

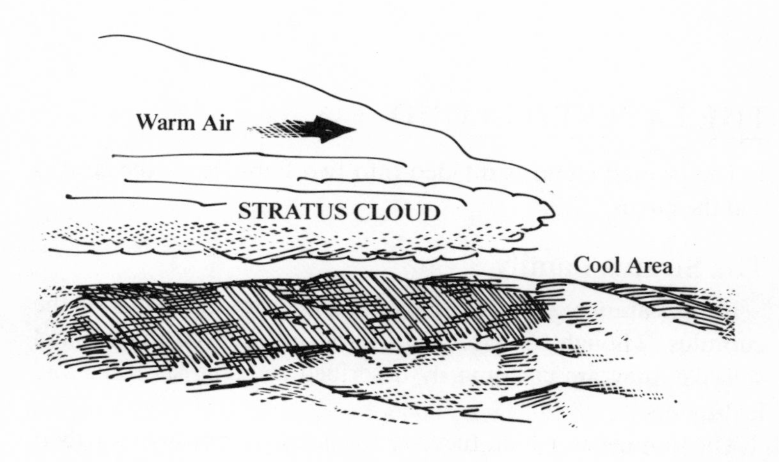

STRATUS CLOUDS *are formed when a layer of warm air moves into a cool area and is cooled to or below its dew point. Stratus clouds are customarily described as being sheetlike and featureless.*

At ground level: stratus, fog
Up to 6,000 feet: stratus, high fog, low cloud
6,000 to around 17,000 feet, with the average cloud base being 10,000 feet: altostratus, middle cloud
17,000 feet and above: cirrostratus, high cloud

And now one of the most imaginative of American Indian predictions:

| *When the sun is in his house, it will rain soon.*

What is being seen here is a pale, shimmering, and veiled look that gives the impression of the sun looming behind a pane of frosted glass or being "in his house." It is caused by the passage of altostratus clouds. The prediction is a sound one because the wind often brings the altostratus in ahead of rain-bearing clouds, with precipitation likely in about 10 to 15 hours.

The Cirrus Family

Members of the cirrus family are all high flyers, with their bases averaging about 20,000 feet above the earth. Formed at such heights, they consist almost entirely of ice droplets. Like stratus clouds, they come into being when a stretch of warmish air is overcome by the cold atmosphere around it.

Cirrus clouds are divided into several groups, with the chief representatives being the cirrus itself and the already mentioned cirrocumulus and cirrostratus.

The cirrus cloud usually takes shape at 25,000 feet or higher; whitish in color, it is thin, wispy, and feathery. The cirrocumulus and cirrostratus are found immediately below the cirrus — at altitudes between 20,000 and 25,000 feet. The cirrocumulus is made up of thin, patchy clouds that often assume wavelike patterns; the cirrostratus forms itself into thin sheets that resemble torn strips of gauze or finely meshed veils.

Mares' tails, mares' tails,
Make lofty ships carry low sails.

This wise old maritime rhyme concerns itself with the wispy cirrus cloud. Over the centuries, its gossamer curls and arcs of white have been described as mares' tails, filly tails, hen scratches, and the light strokes of a painter's brush. The prediction, however, will be reliable only under certain circumstances. The mares' tails promise good weather when idly and gracefully marking the sky here and there. The same applies when their points are turned downward. Dry, calm air makes the downward turns possible.

But, should the tails turn upward, then wind, humidity, and unstable air pressures are at work. These are all signs of the possibility of rain. Also, when a storm is brewing, the cirrus are swiftly blown along miles ahead of the approaching rain. And so, for sailors, the presence of fast-moving and upward-pointing mares' tails was a signal to reduce sail for safety's sake.

The same signal gave birth to these variations:

If the clouds look as if scratched by a hen,
Get ready to reef your sails then.

(The final line can also read:
Be ready to reef your topsails in.)

Hen scratches and filly tails,
Get ready to reef your topsails.

Trace in the sky the painter's brush,
The winds around you soon will rush.

When rain is in the offing, the sky is often painted over with what is called a mackerel sky. This is a patchy, mottled, and sometimes knobby formation of cirrocumulus clouds. The formation indicates that the cirrocumulus are riding a wind that is likely bringing rain-bearing clouds. And so, from the seamen of old, ever alert for the changes in weather that could bode them good or ill, we have:

> *Mackerel scales,*
> *Furl your sails.*

Joined by two cautions from the land:

> *Mackerel scales in the sky,*
> *Expect more wet than dry.*
>
> (The first line can also read:
> *Mackerel clouds in the sky.*)

> *A mackerel sky won't leave the ground dry.*

And these warnings:

> *Mackerel sky,*
> *Not yet wet,*
> *Not yet dry.*

> *A curdly sky is the sign of rain within three days.*
>
> — NEW ENGLAND

Both warnings spring from the cirrocumulus formation often seen moving by in advance of an approaching warm front. Since the front is noted for its casual and slow-moving approach, rain is not yet likely for one or two full days.

The two kinds of clouds, with one coming after the other at times, or appearing together in the sky, have been joined in two proverbs:

Mackerel scales and mares' tails
Make lofty ships carry low sails.

(The opening line can also read:
Mares' tails and mackerel scales or mackerel skies.)

OF POSITION, COLOR, AND ACTION

The weather is not foretold only by the type of cloud that looms overhead or on the horizon. Much of what is to come is presaged by the position, the color, and the actions of the clouds. Over the centuries, all such omens have found their way into the literature of weather lore. Here is a sampling of what the skywatchers have seen and concluded:

The higher the clouds, the better the weather.

(In some areas, the line reads
the finer the weather.)

The proverb, though seeming general in nature, is very restricted in its meaning. It applies to the cumulus cloud only and does not even extend itself to the cumulonimbus. When a pocket of warm air rises from the earth to form the cumulus, it surrenders its heat as it travels. Consequently, the pocket that finally creates an ordinary cumulus at a very high altitude has sacrificed so much of its humidity that the cloud's moisture content is insufficient to produce any appreciable amount of rain or snow. Conversely, a lowering of the clouds is an unmistakable signal that the moisture content is increasing and that rain is more than likely.

> *If clouds be bright,*
> *'Twill clear tonight.*
> *If clouds be dark,*
> *'Twill rain, do you hark?*

Here we have another of weather lore's most obvious entries. Even the world's most casual skywatcher knows from childhood that white clouds suggest fair weather and that, the darker they become, the more they herald rain. What is operative here is the fact that a cloud's luminosity comes from a combination of three sources: light from the sun, light reflected by the particles (dust and so on) within the cloud, and light reflected from the ground. A white cloud, reflecting a great deal of sunlight, indicates a low water count. But, as the cloud fattens with pre-storm moisture, its growing thickness brings to the forefront the reflection of the particles within it and the light reflected from the ground. Its color darkens to an increasingly foreboding shade.

> *When you see a cloud in the sky that grows larger, it is going to storm. When you see a cloud grow smaller and melt away, it is going to be fair.*

> *If the sun shines clear in the early morning and then the sky clouds up, it will rain before night.*

> *Cumulus clouds smaller at sunset than at noon are signs of continued fair weather.*

Once again, we're dealing with the obvious. But, as is true of so much that is obvious, the sayings are worth betting on any day in the week. When clouds grow in size, it is, of course, because their moisture content is increasing. When they shrink, they are surrendering their moisture content to the atmosphere, literally melting away and diminishing the threat of rain.

Now clouds combine, and spread o'er all the sky,
When little rugged parts ascend on high,
Which may be entwined, though by a feeble tie;
These make small clouds, which driven on by wind,
To other like and little clouds are joined,
And these increase by more; at last they form
Thick, heavy clouds; and thence proceeds a storm.

— LUCRETIUS (circa 95–55 B.C.)
From: *De Rerum Natura*

Obviously, when the clouds grow larger before a storm, they steadily fill the sky, closing off our view of the blue vault beyond them. Lucretius may have expressed this fact with memorable eloquence, but the New Englanders of old used just six words to say the same thing:

Open and shet,
Sign of wet.

* * *

When the carry goes west,
Gude weather is past.
When the carry goes east,
Gude weather comes neist.

This is both a wind and cloud proverb. It is basically sound because, in our latitudes, a cloud being carried westward indicates a bad-weather wind from some point in the east, while an eastward-moving cloud indicates a good-weather west wind. But, as you'll recall from the preceding chapter, a west wind can bring every type of weather to some areas, including stretches along the Pacific Coast of the United States.

If the sun sets in a cloud, it will rain on the morrow.

This one, an aged New England saw, is not to be trusted unless the cloud is an extremely large one. If the cloud is small, you might well find yourself looking at the sun in a perfectly clear and fair-weather sky were you to adjust your position some distance to the north or south.

> *The storm alights on the mountain and walks into the valley.*
>
> — NEW ENGLAND

> *When the clouds are upon the hills,*
> *They'll come down by the mills.*

At work here is a meteorological activity that takes place as warmish air travels up the side of a mountain. On moving into higher altitudes along the slopes, it condenses into clouds that then release either rain or snow. The resultant storm can be widespread, extending back down the mountainside. An old and charming English rhyme, without actually mentioning a mountain, speaks of this same activity:

> *When it gangs up i' sops* [small clouds],
> *It'll fall down i' drops.*

On the far side of the mountain, the passing air follows a downward course, steadily heating itself as it works its way through the lower altitudes and eventually causing the clouds to disperse or evaporate. The result: the windward sides of mountains are customarily lush with trees and other vegetation, while the leeward sides are dry and sprinkled here and there with trees. The leeward sides are also subject to hot, dry winds such as the chinooks of the Rockies and the *foehns* of the Alps. Both are capable of melting snow and raising temperatures significantly within a matter of minutes.

The condensation that occurs as warm air moves up the windward slopes can shroud the top of a mountain or a hill with a distinctive layer of cloud. That layer, which the residents thereabouts liken to a cap or some other type of headgear, is a strong indication of rain to come and has resulted in a string of local predictions in diverse areas. Varied though the areas may be, the predictions all sound as if composed by a single cloud watcher. Here, from Great Britain and the United States, are just a few:

> *When Pembroke puts on his cowl,*
> *The Dunion on his hood,*
> *Then a' the wives of Teviotside*
> *Ken there will be a flood.*

— SCOTLAND

> *A cloud on Sidlaw Hills foretells rain to Carmyllie.*

— EASTERN SCOTLAND, NEAR DUNDEE

> *When Lookout Mountain wears cloud caps, it will rain in six hours.*

— WYOMING

> *When Breedon Hill puts on his cap,*
> *Ye men of the vale beware of that.*

— WORCESTERSHIRE, ENGLAND

> *When Cheviot ye see put on his cap,*
> *Of rain ye'll have a wee bit drap.*

— CHEVIOT HILLS, SOUTHERN SCOTLAND

Borne on the winds, the clouds have brought in the rain, and with it some of the most fascinating entries in all of weather lore.

CHAPTER SIX

When Rain Comes

THE CONTRIBUTIONS that rain has brought to weather lore are fascinating and considerable. In the main, they consist of predictions of when rain is to be expected, comments on how long it will hang about once it has put in an appearance, plus an assortment of superstitions on what it forebodes and how it can be summoned or driven away. They all point to one fact. Rain has attracted more attention than any other single weather phenomenon — and for good reason. We have learned only too well through the ages what it can do to every aspect of our daily lives.

PREDICTIONS

Predictions of its visits outweigh by far the other rain proverbs. Ranging from the completely true to the completely false, they come mostly from people who have lived close to the land or sea and have been most vulnerable to the weather and its caprices. They are inventions fashioned from heeding the behavior of the sky, the animals all around, the earth underfoot, household items, and one's own suddenly troublesome teeth or knees.

The Sky

> *The higher the clouds, the better the weather.*

> *When smoke descends, good weather ends.*

These two predictions are variations on the same theme and can be trusted most of the time. High-flying clouds indicate dry air and high atmospheric pressure overhead. Both are fair-weather conditions. Rain, however, is preceded in our latitudes by the low-pressure counterclockwise spiral that renders the atmospheric pressure unstable and generates an increasing humidity. Both factors press down on ascending smoke and finally force it earthward. The atmospheric upheavals that join the humidity in foretokening rain are a lowering air pressure and a shift of the wind to some point from the east. And so one caution must always be kept in mind. The rising humidity may be very noticeable, but you'll risk a mistake if you predict a shower or downpour when high humidity is not accompanied by its fellow conditions. Although humidity does presage a change in the weather, it does not, by itself, necessarily signal the approach of rain. It can just as well announce the arrival of an overcast sky.

The forces responsible for the above twosome are also behind this antique sea chant:

> *The farther the sight,*
> *The nearer the rain.*

The sailors of old knew what they were talking about here. Distant objects have a way of appearing hazy in good weather but of suddenly sharpening when bad weather is afoot. The change is prompted by the pre-storm wind shift, and what happens is this: when a high pressure, good-weather system is on hand, your visibility is limited because the air is fairly static and thus filled with dust. Then in comes a low pressure system with its backing wind and humidity. The air thins and the dust scatters. Not only do you now see farther and more clearly, but distant objects give the impression of drawing closer as well.

Seamen are not the only ones to have noticed the telltale change in visibility. Many a farmer has picked out distant hills or trees for daily watching and has predicted a fair or rainy sky on how clearly they can be seen. Though not a farmer, Aristotle also recognized this phenomenon and wrote that when "the cliffs and promontories of the shore appear higher and the dimensions of all objects seem larger, then the southeast wind is blowing."

There's more to this, however. Your hearing as well as your vision is improved: in fair weather, sound waves travel upward and outward into the atmosphere, there to be dissipated; but on a cloudy, humid day, they are bent back to earth, with the result that their range is considerably extended. The fact that distant roaring streams, singing birds, and the crack of an ax on wood all sound nearer is behind this old British rhyme:

> *Sound traveling far and wide*
> *A stormy day this doth betide.*

Colors

Now we come to some of the best-known proverbs — those referring to the color of the sky at sunset and dawn. They are predictions based on the various colors that come to the forefront as the sunlight, white to begin with, splits itself into the bands of the color spectrum. This occurs when the sunlight ricochets off the water vapor and foreign particles — dust, soot, and the like — in the atmosphere. Of all the hues, red has invited the most attention down through the centuries.

This collection of proverbs resembles the red sun prophecies discussed in Chapter Two, which also deal with the sunset and the dawn. These are the times when the sun is low to the horizon, where the air is most thickly concentrated. That heavy concentration breaks up the shorter color wavelengths and allows only the longest wavelengths — those at the red end of the spectrum —to break through.

There, however, the similarity between the two types of proverbs ends. Though you'll find that their dawn predictions are in agreement, their sunset proverbs contradict each other. A sun with a red face at the close of day promises rain. But a red sky at sunset foretells something quite different, as can be seen in these various comments known the world over:

> *When it is evening, ye say, it will be fair weather:*
> *For the sky is red.*
> *And, in the morning, it will be foul weather today:*
> *For the sky is lowering.*

— MATTHEW XVI: 2-3

> *Red sky at night, sailor's delight.*
> *Red sky in the morning, sailor's warning.*

— MARITIME SAYING

> *Red sky at night, shepherd's delight.*
> *Red sky in the morning, shepherd's warning.*

— LANDLUBBER'S VERSION

> *Evening red and weather fine,*
> *Morning red, of rain's a sign.*

> *Like a red morn, that ever yet betokened*
> *Wreck to the seaman, tempest to the field,*
> *Sorrow to shepherds, woe unto the birds,*
> *Gust and foul flaws to herdmen and to herds.*

— SHAKESPEARE
From: *Venus and Adonis*

Why the disagreement with the red sun forecasts? Much of the trouble stems from the word "red" itself. When the red sky forecasters wrote their predictions, they were probably thinking of various shades of pink and likely substituted red for the sake of convenience and dramatic effect. The lighter reds in the spectrum take shape when the sunlight is passing through a high concentration of dust particles — namely, through the high pressure, stable air that is associated with fair weather. When they are seen late in the day, the sun is sending its light through good-weather air that lies between us and its descent in the west. Thus, with the weather in our latitudes approaching on a westerly wind, we can pretty well count on a fair day tomorrow.

But, on the other hand, the red sun proverbs refer to a fiery hue. That deep red, you'll recall, is caused by a heavy concentration of water vapor in the atmosphere. Hence, rain is predicted.

Everything shifts into reverse for the red sky predictions when morning arrives. Ascending in the east, the sun is now shining through dusty air that, again because of our westerly winds, is being eased out of our area. An increasing humidity will often follow from the west, giving rise to the possibility of anything from unsettled conditions to rain. As for the red sun in the morning, its fiery appearance continues to foretoken rain.

Of the two types of red sky predictions, the sunset ones are the more reliable. They speak of a definite kind of approaching weather. The morning forecasts look at a departing weather and depend for their accuracy on the conditions that can be normally — but not necessarily — expected to follow it.

Although the color red is mentioned most often, purple, green, and gray also appear in weather lore forecasts:

> *But if with purple rays he* [the sun] *brings the light,*
> *And a pure heaven resigns to quiet night,*
> *No rising winds or falling storms are nigh.*

— VIRGIL

> *Glimpse you e'er the green ray,*
> *Count the morrow a fine day.*

> *Gray evening sky,*
> *Not one day dry.*

Why are these colors such reliable forecasters? Blue (caused by a medium and balanced concentration of water vapor and dust particles) predominates in daytime fair weather. If the blue remains at dusk or deepens to purple with the coming dark, the amiable mood of the day can be expected to linger for a time to come. Green also suggests an atmosphere without too heavy a water content and implies a continuation of good weather. It is often seen as a final flash of light just before the sun finally disappears. Hence, in its proverb, it is called the green ray.

Yellow, too, indicates good weather — an atmosphere not heavily laden with water vapor. But you need to be a bit cautious with your predictions here and watch for two kinds of yellow sky. Each foretells its own brand of weather. A bright yellow can mean a fair but windy tomorrow. A white-yellow, especially if it arcs high across the vault of the sky, may threaten rain.

Gray works with the sunlight much as red does, but achieves an exact opposite effect. Evening gray lets us know the sun is shining through a wettish air mass approaching from the west and promising rain, probably by tomorrow. (You'll recall from Chapter Two that a "gray-faced" or pale sun late in the day likewise promises rain.) Conversely, a gray dawn means that the watery air is moving out of our neighborhood, with good weather likely arriving to take its place.

Some wise heads long ago noted the similar but diametrically opposed messages delivered by the red and gray skies and tied the two in a number of prophecies:

Evening red and morning gray
Sends the traveler on his way.
Evening gray and morning red
Sends the traveler wet to bed.

(In certain areas, the final line reads:
Brings down rain upon his head.)

If the evening is red and the morning gray,
It is the sign of a bonnie day.
If the evening is gray and the morning red,
The lamb and ewe will go wet to bed.

A red evening and a gray morning
Set the pilgrim a-walking.

Evening red and morning gray,
Two sure signs of one fine day.

Or as quoted by Sir Humphrey Davy in *Salmonia:*

The evening red and the morning gray,
Is the sure sign of a fair day.

Animals

Blessed with some physical sensibilities obviously keener than ours and governed by instincts that seem able to outdo the most finely tuned ESP, animals are fine weather barometers and have been used as such by man, perhaps from the very day that he started watching them. In his watching, he's dreamed up enough animal weather proverbs to fill this entire chapter. In fact, name just about any animal that you can think of and the chances are that you'll find it to be the subject of an old saying or verse somewhere in the world.

Sea gull, sea gull, sitting on the sand,
Rain is due when you're at hand.

(The final line often reads:
It's a sign of rain when you're at hand.)

Swallows fly low before a rain.

If the robin sings in the bush,
Then the weather will be coarse.
If the robin sings on the barn,
Then the weather will be warm.

Flies bite more before a rain.

When horses sweat in the barn,
It is a sign of rain.

When black snails on the road you see,
Then on the morrow rain will be.

If bees stay at home,
Rain will soon come.
If they fly away,
Fine will be the day.

All these predictions are pretty much on the mark. To begin, sea gulls, along with most other birds, tend to settle down somewhere in the hours before a storm. It may be that they're sensibly protecting themselves or, as might be the case with the robin, safeguarding their nests. And it is likely that the pre-storm drop in barometric pressure, thinning the air as it does, is making it too difficult for them to support themselves aloft.

Swallows (in common with many other animals, among them bats) are blessed with ears sensitive to changes in air pressure.

When the pressure drops before a storm, they feel a discomfort and fly close to the earth where the pressure still remains somewhat high.

Flies, gnats, mosquitoes, fleas, and any number of other insects likewise seem to find flying difficult at the approach of wet weather and so tend to swarm and cling to the things about them, including the human body. Their pestering and biting ways may also be the result of an irritability caused by the changing atmospheric conditions. But we ourselves have to take some of the blame for the bites. The decreasing air pressure enables more odors, all of them inviting, to be released from our bodies. Then the increasing humidity causes us to sweat and provides the fly and his fellow insects with what, to them, is a gourmet dish.

Horses (and other animals) perspire as do humans when the humidity increases. And anyone who has a garden knows that snails are out in the open and underfoot in startling numbers during wet weather or its approach. It's just the way they are.

Finally, as any beekeeper will testify, his charges are excellent forecasters. At the first approach of foul weather, they customarily neither swarm aimlessly nor settle on anyone's hide. Rather, as the humidity rises, they head for the hive and remain safe and dry inside throughout the storm. Only when the rain is definitely past do they once more venture outside. Their prudence has inspired many a now-antique weather proverb:

When bees to distance wing their flight
Days are warm and skies are bright.
But when their flight ends near their home,
Stormy weather is sure to come.

A swarm of bees in July
Does little more than bring a dry.

When bees stay close by the hive,
Rain is close by.

A bee was never caught in a shower.

When charged with stormy matter lower the skies,
The busy bee at home her labor plies.

— ARATUS

A bee's wings never get wet.

Fascinating as they may be, not all forecasts based on animal behavior are to be trusted. While some are quite accurate, others are vigorously questioned by weather lorists, while still others have been dismissed as pure fancy. The fault here lies with the observer rather than the animals. Too often down through the centuries, farmers have seen one of their animals, say a cow, pull some odd stunt, such as rubbing its hind quarters against a fence, at the hint of a storm. After two or three encore performances, they've nodded sagely and have passed the word on to their neighbors. And lo! A mistaken universal has been born. The singular behavior of one animal has been extended to an entire breed — and, despite all scientific opinion to the contrary, has stubbornly remained in widespread belief ever since.

Whether the forecasts are accurate or not, their fascination remains — a testament, on the one hand, to man's perception and imagination and, on the other, to his fallibility as he continually attempts to make all those connections that enable him to comprehend a little more the intricacies and mysteries of nature. Here, accompanied by notes on the degree of their validity, are a representative few of the connections man has actually made or has imagined he has made:

An open ant hill indicates good weather;
A closed one, an approaching storm.

Seems to be true. Ants have often been observed building and fortifying their nests as rain approaches. They finish the job off by closing the mouth of the nest. All this activity has also led to the belief that the presence of fresh earth on or around an ant nest signals rain.

> *When buffalo band together,*
> *The storm god is herding them.*

This is an American Indian saying. It's likely true, with the animals, perhaps made nervous by the changing weather, coming together for a sense of comfort, not to mention some measure of protection from the elements. European sheepherders of old saw the same tendency in their flocks and came up with:

> *When sheep collect and huddle,*
> *Tomorrow will become a puddle.*

The rhyme seems a clever one until we realize that it may have been borrowed from a proverb mentioned in Chapter Three:

> *When the stars begin to huddle,*
> *The earth will soon become a puddle.*

Or perhaps the borrowing was the other way around.

> *Wild geese, wild geese going out to sea,*
> *All fine weather it will be.*

> *She* [the goose] *is no witch, or astrologer, to divine by the starries, but yet hath a shrewd guess of rainie weather, being as good as an almanack to some that believe in her.*

— ENGLAND (circa 1600s)

Is the goose an accurate forecaster? Small-boat fishermen in New England apparently think so. Before sailing out for the day, they are said to look skyward to check the flight of geese and sea gulls. If they glimpse the birds heading seaward, they follow close behind, reasonably certain that the coming hours will be fair. Should they see the birds wheel inland, their boats remain at anchor.

But now we're in for a little difficulty. Note the following contradictions:

> *Near the surface, quick to bite,*
> *Catch your fish when rain's in sight.*

> *Fish bite the least,*
> *With wind in the east.*
> (Remember, an east wind is a bad-weather wind.)

Both salt and fresh-water fish tend to move closer to the surface in the hours before a storm, perhaps driven there by an alteration in the water's oxygen distribution prompted by the change in air pressure. But do they bite with greater or less enthusiasm than usual? The answer depends on the fisherman you happen to ask. One will insist that fish will take your bait more quickly before than after a storm. Another will claim that they'll ignore you and spend their time snapping at the flies that venture close to the water. So take your pick. But one thing does seem likely about the second proverb: it probably refers to severe thunderstorms. They are known to render fish less active, and thus less eager to bite.

You'll also get an argument on these:

> *Grumphie smells the weather,*
> *An' Grumphie sees the wun'* [wind];
> *He kens when clouds will gather,*
> *And smoor the blinkin' sun.*

— England

> *When ants travel in a straight line, expect rain.*
> *When they scatter, expect fair weather.*

Dogs eat grass before a rain.

When the rooster crows at night,
He tells you that rain's in sight.

or

If the cock crows going to bed,
He wakens with a watery head.

"Grumphie" is a pig, an animal that farmers throughout the world have credited with a particularly keen sensitivity for approaching storms, insisting that he (or she) becomes highly agitated at the first sign of trouble and further claiming that the pig is even able to smell the yet-to-fall rain. Their admiration for the animal's sense of smell can perhaps be traced back to the Roman poet Virgil, who wrote of pigs "tossing their snouts" when a storm was in the air. Many weather lorists today, while agreeing that changing weather may disturb the pig as much as other animals, seriously doubt its olfactory talents. A great many farmers would argue against their skepticism.

The idea that ants (and other bugs) move in a straight line rather than scurrying here and there when bad weather is at hand has long been doubted. Though some ants have been seen on the march as rain is approaching, just as many others have been sighted hurrying along in tidy lines to and from some cupboard treasure in good weather.

As for dogs eating grass: more doubt. This dietary habit is widely dismissed as nonsense, but there is a suspicion that the forecast may apply at least to old, rheumatic dogs. Feeling pained and ill by the humidity and atmospheric changes, they may instinctively turn to the grass as a means of purging their discomfort by vomiting. Perhaps. Whatever the case, some two hundred years ago, one ardent British naturalist, Dr. Edward Jenner

(1749–1823), noted his own pet's odd pre-storm behavior and wrote of it in a poem now familiar to many weather lorists, "Signs of Rain":

> *My dog, so altered in his taste,*
> *Quits mutton bones on grass to feast.*

Respected though he is as an amateur naturalist, Jenner is better known for his medical accomplishments. He developed the world's first workable tuberculosis vaccine.

And the crowing rooster: still more doubt. The best that can be said is that some of his kind do set up a racket and some don't. When a rooster does crow, many farmers and weather lorists believe that he's been disturbed and wakened by the decreasing air pressure and rising humidity. If so, he may well be sharing a discomfort with three other animals noted for their pre-storm vocalizing:

> *When the ass doth bray,*
> *Be sure we shall have rain that day.*

> *When the peacock loudly bawls,*
> *Soon we'll have both rain and squalls.*

> *The bob white sings before a storm.*

Some New Englanders insist that the bob white is warning, "More wet. More wet."

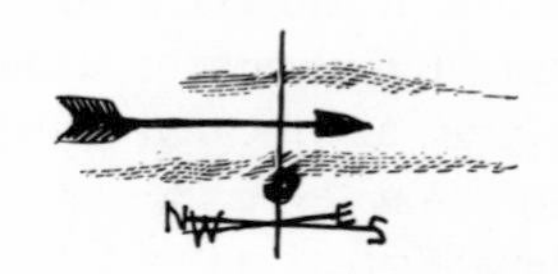

The Earth

Pimpernel, pimpernel, tell me true
Whether the weather be fine or no.

— ENGLAND

Trees grow dark before a storm.

When the leaves show their backs, rain comes.

When leaves show their undersides,
Be sure that rain betides.

The silver maple shows the lining of its leaves before a storm.

The pimpernel rhyme is not itself a prediction but a recognition of this delicate plant's forecasting abilities. When the pre-rain humidity reaches 80%, the pimpernel closes its leaves, forming itself into its own raincoat. It is a method of self-protection that the pimpernel shares with many other plants — dandelions, tulips, clover, laurels, and milkweed, to name just a few.

There is nothing protective, however, in the darkening of trees prior to a rain. At work here is the landscape's habit of reflecting the sky. In this instance, the trees are reflecting the dark rain clouds and are themselves giving the impression of darkening.

The pre-rain wind is responsible for making leaves foretell a storm by showing their backs, undersides, or linings. Leaves grow with their topsides pressed back by the prevailing wind. When the wind shifts before a storm, it strikes the undersides of the leaves, curls them forward, and temporarily transforms them into the topsides.

Storms burst as the tide turns.

> *Showers are most frequent when the tide turns.*

Behind these two very accurate predictions is the pre-storm drop in air pressure. It is a decrease capable of adjusting a water level significantly, causing it to rise by a foot or more. When the pressure drops, the air thins and lessens its suppressive grip on the water surface. The water is able to rise and, in turn, the tide rises, or flows. Conversely, when the pressure again increases in the wake of a storm, down comes that invisible, suppressive grip. The tide ebbs.

As accurate as the two predictions are, they can be trusted only when certain conditions apply. They won't work if the joint solar and lunar influences on the tide are in opposition to and more powerful than those of the coming storm.

> *Seaweed dry, sunny sky.*
> *Seaweed wet, rain you'll get.*

— NEW ENGLAND

> *Moss dry, sunny sky.*
> *Moss wet, rain you'll get.*

— SOUTHERN U.S. VERSION

Seaweed and moss do a very efficient job of absorbing moisture. Consequently, both become noticeably wet in the pre-rain humidity. Tobacco and hemp react in similar fashion and can serve as reliable forecasters.

> *When the ditch and pond offend the nose,*
> *Then look for rain and stormy blows.*

Very true. Dirt, mud, and stagnant water all contain decaying organic matter whose odors are kept in check by high air pressure. But, just as a lowering air pressure enables our bodies to release those odors so attractive to flying insects, so does it permit the odors to escape from ditches, ponds, and swamps.

Sounds

> *A rising well and a gushing spring*
> *Are two good signs of the very same thing*
> [bad weather].

Equally true. Many wells and springs do indeed rise in the pre-storm hours, with both capable of producing an energetic, gushing sound. What is going on is this: an underground water channel or chamber dries up to one extent or another during fair weather, leaving some water at its exit point. Air and other gases flow into the empty space, there to be trapped and held in place because their pressure is in balance with the air pressure on the far side of the water at the exit. Then comes the pre-storm drop in air pressure. The trapped air and gases are able to drive out into a well or spring whatever water is present in the channel or chamber. In some instances, the process creates a stream of bubbles that produces the gushing sound.

The natural materials in homes react along with the earth and begin to produce some storm-associated phenomena of their own. For one, it was widely believed in England and colonial America that:

> *When soot falls down the chimney, rain is near.*

If there is truth here, then the changing air pressure and rising humidity are at work. Normal air pressure, along with dryness and a certain amount of atmospheric magnetism, is believed to hold the soot in place during good weather. When the pressure decreases and the dryness disappears, the soot is free to break loose and drop into the hearth. An accelerating wind may also share some of the responsibility. To veteran New Englanders, a "whistling wind" around the house is a dead certain sign of rain.

Then there are all the other pre-storm sounds familiar to us. Walls creak with the wind and rising humidity. Burning logs pop as the descending air pressure releases the moisture within them. Wood furniture, as Jenner noted in "Signs of Rain," adds its share to the noise:

> *Hark how the chairs and tables crack!*

The furniture also begins to "sweat" as the lowering air pressure enables polishing oils to come to the surface. Soap did the same thing in the days when it was made at home. Especially at the end of a prolonged dry spell, the humidity gathered quickly on its surface and resulted in this prophecy:

> *When drops collect on soap,*
> *For rainfall you can hope.*

The Human Body

There's no need to tell anyone with corns, bunions, rheumatism, a cranky tooth, an old surgical scar, or a creak in the knee or some other joint that a change for the worse in the weather can bring on its fair share of aches and pains. Nor is there a need to tell many people of the sadness, depression, or sudden burst of temperament that a dark day can induce. Doing the job in either case, of course, are the mounting humidity and the lowering air pressure, both of which are able to prompt physical and emotional upsets that, depending on the individual, can prove to be anything from slightly bothersome to downright uncomfortable. Human hair absorbs moisture in pre-rain humidity, so much so that long ago the American Indians, on looking at some prized souvenirs, had this to say:

> *When locks in the scalp house turn limp,*
> *It will rain on the morrow.*

Human hair does such a good job of soaking up moisture and turning limp in the process that it is employed in the hygrometer, the gauge used for measuring humidity. For some reason, blond hair is especially sensitive to the increasing wetness and is preferred in the hygrometer.

Because bodily discomforts depend on the individual, they have not been the source of many proverbs, which are intended as universal truths. Of the few that have become proverbs, the best known include:

> *Old Betty's nerves are on the rack.*
>
> — JENNER
> From: "Signs of Rain"

> *A coming storm your shooting corns presage,*
> *And aches will throb, your hollow tooth will rage.*
> *Sauntering in coffee house is Dulman seen;*
> *He damns the climate and complains of spleen.*
>
> — JONATHAN SWIFT (1667–1745)
> From: "Rain"

> *As old sinners have all points*
> *O' the compass in their bones and joints.*
>
> — SAMUEL BUTLER (1612–1680)

> *The minds of men do in the weather share,*
> *Dark or serene as the day's foul or fair.*
>
> — CICERO (106–43 B.C.)

> *So it falls that all men are*
> *With fine weather happier far.*
>
> — KING ALFRED (circa 848–899)

RAIN IN THE MAKING

Rain, rain, go away,
Come again some other day.

Rain, rain, go to Spain,
And never come here again.

— BRITISH

Rain, rain, go away,
Come again tomorrow day.
When I brew and when I bake,
I'll give you a little cake.

Just what is this phenomenon — this rain — that attracts such human interest and is responsible for so much of the world's weather lore? Where does it come from? How does it take shape? To begin with you need clouds. They are a must for the production of rain. Made up of water droplets or ice particles, clouds are the world's single carriers of the airborne moisture that falls as rain. But the water droplets within a cloud must reach a certain size before gravity can pull them earthward.

The cloud-making process begins with the sun's causing moisture to evaporate from the earth's surface. The moisture rises through the atmosphere until it reaches an altitude where colder air cools it to or below its dew point — the point on nature's thermometer at which the wetness begins to condense and become visible, turning itself into countless tiny droplets. (Actually, tiny is too conservative a word for the droplets. Microscopic is a better choice.)

Clinging to specks of dust, bits of airborne minerals, and traces of salt from the sea and elsewhere, the droplets cluster together and form themselves into clouds. These droplets bounce about in the atmosphere, rise and fall with the various air currents, and travel in their cloud over vast distances. The one thing they can't yet do is fall as rain. They are too small and weightless for gravity to take over and pull them down through the drafts on which they are riding. To be able to fall as rain, a droplet has to increase in size. Then it takes on a pear shape, surrenders to gravity, and falls as rain.

Patterns of Growth

The cloud that promises rain is a thing of action. We see some of that action as the winds sweep the cloud overhead. But the crucial part of the action occurs within the cloud and is invisible to our eyes. There, caught in the harsh updrafts of warm, moist air that create the rain cloud (and then the accompanying downdrafts that are generated when warm and cold air meet), the droplets are in constant motion, colliding and embracing to form droplets of increasing size. This process is called coalescence, a thoroughly drab term for a passionate and often violent activity.

Coalescence is known to occur in two ways. The type that takes place as you look skyward depends on a number of factors, especially the air temperature within the clouds. If you're in a warm area at the time, especially a tropical zone, the droplets are of varying sizes. The larger of the lot move more slowly in the disturbed atmosphere than do their smaller companions, with some heavy enough to fall to lower levels within their cloud. Their slow movement and descent send them into the paths of the smaller droplets. Now comes the collision and embrace. The process repeats itself until the ballooning droplets are large enough to fall as rain.

But let there be lower air temperatures and the second type of coalescence comes into play. This type occurs in clouds that extend into altitudes where the temperatures run well below the freezing mark — from about -4°F. down to around -40°F. In delicate balance within the clouds are ice crystals, water vapor, and supercooled water droplets (meaning droplets that, despite the low temperature, are not frozen). It is a balance that cannot be maintained for long because of the conflicting actions taken by the droplets and crystals at these temperatures.

What happens is this: at the start the water droplets are stable because the air is saturated with water vapor, meaning that no further water can be evaporated into the air. In turn, this means that the rate at which water molecules are being evaporated at the earth's surface is the same as the rate at which they are condensing within the cloud. For the droplets, everything is nicely in balance. But, for the ice crystals, the air is supersaturated; there is too much water present and so they begin to absorb some of it. But, as the vapor disappears, the water droplets attempt to restore the initial balance by themselves evaporating — only to turn into a vapor that freezes on the crystals, causing a further growth that ultimately sends the crystals earthward as snow. On descending through warmer altitudes, they melt when the temperature reaches 32°F. and travel the rest of the way down as rain. If the lower-altitude temperature remains below the freezing mark, the crystals land as snow.

Far more complex than its counterpart, this second type of coalescence is responsible for most of the rain that falls in the temperate latitudes, ours among them. It is operative above much of the United States.

HOW LONG THE RAIN?

We began this chapter with a string of predictions on when rain can be expected. It's time now to sample those that prophesy how long it will remain once on the scene.

> *If the rain waits till noon to visit,*
> *Prepare for a long visit.*

The saying applies to weather borne on a warm front. That front, you'll recall from Chapter Four, spends a long while overhead before losing its rain.

> *Rain before seven,*
> *Clear by eleven.*
>
> (The second line may also read:
> *Fine before eleven* or *Shine before eleven.*)

This is a hit or miss proposition, proving itself correct perhaps 50% of the time. It's bound to work on occasion because so many rains last but briefly, usually no more than 4 or 5 hours. And so an early morning shower can be expected to depart sometime prior to noon — that is, unless a warm front is in play overhead. New Englanders have an imaginative but down-to-earth variation on the prediction:

> *Morning rain is like an old lady's dance.*
> *It doesn't last very long.*

Next:

> *A sunshiny shower won't last out the hour.*

The proverb is based on the fact that, when the sunlight can be seen, the rain is falling from a small cloud that will soon pass on, taking its wetness with it. Proverbs, as we'll see momentarily, are also used to predict the end of a storm.

Here now is one of the most venerable bits of British folklore. It dates back to at least the 1600s.

> *If it rains on Swithin's Day, it will rain for forty days.*

Or, in a much older form:

> *St. Swithin's day, if thou dost rain,*
> *For forty days it will remain;*
> *St. Swithin's day, if thou be fair,*
> *For forty days 'twill rain na mair* [no more].

Venerable though it is, the forecast is totally without substance. Though the hard-to-get-along-with English climate can be counted upon to have wet down some spot in the country on many a St. Swithin's Day (July 15), there is no reliable record of any such rain ever hanging about for more than a month. But no one seems bothered by this. The saying, with its mention of forty days undoubtedly reflecting back to Biblical times, remains alive and well in both England and the United States, recited most of the time in the spirit of good fun, but sometimes with an unthinking seriousness.

All that can be said for the prediction is that it springs from one of the most interesting stories in folklore. It seems that St. Swithin (a 9th-century Anglo-Saxon cleric who became the Bishop of Winchester) so revered the rain as one of God's finest creations that he asked to be buried outdoors so that he could enjoy it throughout eternity. The bishop's request was honored on his death in 862 (circa), but on a July 15 some years later, an attempt was made to place his body inside his church. If the story is to be believed, a great rainstorm immediately burst upon the scene and lasted for 40 days, causing such upset that the transfer was delayed for another century. One of the earliest mentions of the prediction — if not the earliest — is to be found in *Poor Robin's Almanack* of 1697. The good saint also played a part in the life of long-ago apple farmers. They believed that:

> *Rain on St. Swithin's Day or St. Peter's Day* [June 29] *promised a good crop because the two were watering the orchards.*

Actually, folklore abounds with predictions based on a given day's weather conditions. Like the St. Swithin forecast, they are all fascinating — and all quite groundless. A sampling:

> *If St. Vitus Day* [June 15] *be rainy weather,*
> *It will rain for thirty days together.*
>
> — Poor Robin's Almanack, 1697

> *If it rains on July 26th, it will rain for the next two weeks. If it is dry, expect two weeks of dryness.*

> *If St. Paul's Day* [January 25] *be fair and clear,*
> *It will betide a happy year.*

> *If the 24th of August be fair and clear,*
> *Then hope for a prosperous autumn that year.*

The 12 days immediately following Christmas predict the kinds of weather that will be seen throughout the new year. In order, each day's weather will indicate the weather for the corresponding month. Rain on the first day foretokens a rainy January, wind on the second day promises a windy February, and so on.

And, in closing, the delightful:

> *If it rains on or about St. Mary Magdalen's Day* [July 22], *she is washing her kerchief to have it clean and ready for the festival on St. James the Great Day* [July 25].
> (James is Mary's cousin.)

We've seen predictions for how long the rain will last, but when can it be expected to depart? New Englanders and others along the Atlantic coast have long had at least one answer:

> *Enough blue sky in the west for a Dutchman's breeches gives the storm just half an hour.*

What's being seen here are patches of open sky through scudding, broken clouds. They often come at the rear of a low pressure system and are good indications that fair weather is being carried to us on our friendly west winds. The saying is varied in several locales, with a sailor's trousers, a Scot's kilts, and, in the American midwest, a woman's apron being substituted for the Dutchman's breeches. Similar to it are forecasts which hold that clouds, when small or scattering, are breaking up and ending the storm. First, a repeat from earlier in this chapter:

> *A sunshiny shower won't last out the hour.*

And then:

> *If the sun beyond the clouds is blue,*
> *Be glad, there is a picnic for you.*

There are some grains of truth in the two sayings. Patches of open sky often do signal the end of a storm. But they are not to be taken as gospel. It's always wise to remember a basic fact — that storms can and do fool us with temporary respites, showing stretches of blue that will soon be closed over with new rain-bearing clouds. It will be of help to keep those half-dozen New England words from Chapter Five in mind here. They work just as well for the rebirth of a storm as for its birth:

Open and shet,
Signs of wet.

And, as an extra precaution, this aged British advice:

Bright rain makes fools fain.

RAIN AND SUPERSTITION

To the ancients, rain was a sacred gift, perhaps the most sacred of gifts because it was vital to the survival of all life. In addition, for many cultures, it symbolized the spiritual forces that were sent from the heavens to control and guide the life on earth. And, because it came from the heavens, it was to all a symbol of purity — and thus, in turn, a symbol of truth and wisdom. Conversely, because of its power to destroy with its floods on the one hand and its absence on the other, it also symbolized destruction, disease, tyranny, and accident.

Early mythology is punctuated throughout with tales of the rain and its cause. Chinese myth speaks of rain as being the tears that flow from two lovestruck spirits — the Cowherd and the Spinning Maid — when they must part each year. Tales from other cultures are not quite so romantic, for rain was considered by some to be the sweat of their gods. American Indian legend has it that rain is the form in which one's ancestors return to earth.

Down through the centuries, rain has been a rich source not only of myth but also of superstition. In keeping with its moody skies, many of the rain superstitions are not of a particularly happy nature, as witness:

> *A rainy wedding day*
> *Makes the sky of marriage gray.*

or

> *If it rains the day you wed,*
> *It is a sign many tears you'll shed.*
>
> (The final line sometimes reads:
> *It is a sign many tears will be shed.*)

> *Kill a beetle and it will rain.*

> *Kill a snake and hang it high for rain.*
> *Kill a snake and bury it for good weather.*

— EARLY NEW ENGLAND AND BLACK AMERICAN BELIEF

> *Step on an ant and there will be rain.*

At times, the gloom has a touch of humor to it:

> *If the sun shines when it is raining, the devil is beating his wife.*
>
> (In some areas, the saying is extended to include the "fact" that the beating is being done with a codfish.)

> *If you see a dog eating grass and don't wish for a rain, send your children out to chase the animal away. The threatening rain will leave with him.*

To dispel some of the gloom, here is an entertaining bit of European lore. It calls for your participation in a weather activity on New Year's Day. You're to scoop out an onion for each month of the newly arrived year and sprinkle salt into the holes. Then, 12 days later, you're to check your handiwork. The onions in which the salt has dissolved represent the months in which there will be rain. It doesn't mean a thing, but it can be fun to do with the kids. Though born in Europe, the superstition came early to the United States and is widely known here.

Certain of the superstitions can further dispel the gloom. For example, in a number of European areas, rain that fell on religious feast days was believed to have supernatural healing powers; its efficacy was lost, however, if it was not caught as it fell from the sky but was allowed to touch some natural or manmade object on the ground, such as a tree or a roof. A Welsh belief was that babies washed in rainwater began to speak at an earlier-than-usual age.

Of course, since rain is so vital to the crops on which life depends, the history of weather lore is filled with superstitions on what must be done to have the skies release their bounty in times of drought. Here, from Europe and dating back as far as the Middle Ages, are a representative four:

> *Cut or burn a fern.*

> *Throw flour into a spring and then stir the water*
> *with a hazel branch. The mixing will cause a mist*
> *to rise and become a raincloud.*
>
> — FRANCE

> *Dip the statues of saints in water. By doing this, you*
> *will be pleading for rain or punishing the saints for*
> *allowing the drought to continue for so long despite*
> *your many prayers for relief.*

> *Sprinkle water on stones while reciting certain magical prayers.*

These old practices may strike us as naive and bring on a smile. But it's wise not to grin too broadly, for we're not above a few rain superstitions ourselves in this day and age of advanced thinking and technology:

> *Wash the car and it's sure to rain.*

> *You always get rained on when you don't have an umbrella.*

> *It always rains more on the weekends and your days off.*

* * *

To close, we return to Edward Jenner and his classic lines of personal forecasting. Written in 1810 when a lady asked if it would rain on the morrow, his observations embrace so many folk predictions that it seems only right to let him have the last word. The poem, which is also known as "Signs of the Weather," has appeared through the years in several versions of varying lengths. The following is a compilation of three of them.

> *The hollow winds begin to blow;*
> *The clouds look black, the grass is low:*
> *The soot falls down, the spaniels sleep,*
> *And spiders from their cobwebs peep.*
> *Last night the sun went pale to bed,*
> *The moon in halos hid her head;*
> *The boding shepherd heaves a sigh,*
> *For see, a rainbow spans the sky.*

The walls are damp, the ditches smell,
Closed is the pink-eyed pimpernel.
The squalid toads at dusk were seen
Slowly crawling o'er the green;
Loud quack the ducks, the peacocks cry,
The distant hills are looking nigh;
Hark, how the chairs and tables crack!
Old Betty's nerves are on the rack;
And see yon rooks, how odd their flight,
They imitate the gliding kite,
Or seem precipitate to fall
As if they felt the piercing ball;
How restless are the snorting swine,
The busy flies disturb the kine,
Low o'er the grass the swallow wings,
The cricket too, how sharp he sings!
Puss on the hearth, with velvet paws,
Sits wiping her whiskered jaws;
Through the clear streams the fishes rise,
And nimbly catch the incautious flies.
The glowworms numerous and light,
Illumined the dewy dell last night;
The whirling dust the wind obeys,
And in the rapid eddy plays;
The frog has changed his yellow vest,
And in a russet coat is dressed.
Though June, the air is cold and still,
The mellow blackbird's voice is shrill;
My dog, so altered in his taste,
Quits mutton bones on grass to feast;
'Twill surely rain: I see with sorrow,
Our jaunt must be put off to-morrow.

CHAPTER SEVEN

Another Rain, Other Moistures

IN THIS CHAPTER, we're going to be talking of atmospheric moistures, of which snow is the only member of the rain family. The others, though often mistakenly thought of as types of rain, are quite separate phenomena and not fashioned in the manner that rain is.

SNOW

In meteorology, rain is classed as precipitation, meaning simply that it is a moisture that falls to the ground from the clouds. Listed with it in the same family are drizzle, snow, freezing rain, and hail. Of their number, only snow has become the subject of various folk predictions and superstitions over the years, so we will focus on it.

The two processes that make rain — (1) the condensation of water vapor followed by the adventure of collision and coalescence, and (2) the presence of water and ice particles in a supercooled cloud, with the water droplets evaporating and the ice crystals growing — are responsible for snow. The temperature of the cloud also has an effect. In general, that temperature must fall to somewhere between 10°F. and -40°F. before the ice crystals that will land on earth as snow can take shape.

The crystals are formed in either of two ways: by water vapor collecting and freezing on bits of atmospheric dross (bits of soil, ash, or sand, for example) or by water vapor at particularly high and cold altitudes, evaporating directly into crystals.

Once formed, the crystals begin their journey earthward, growing larger as they collect additional evaporating vapor and, just as if they were swelling raindrops, collide and coalesce with other crystals, and fall as snow. However, if the temperature near ground level is above the freezing mark — in most instances, around or upwards of 40°F. — the crystals will melt and land as rain.

Depending on the atmospheric conditions, the crystals are able to assume a variety of forms, appearing as needles, columns, plates, or dendrites. When the air is very moist, they may arrive as needles. With dry air, they are likely to present themselves as columns cast loose from the front of a tiny ice palace.

The plate and dendrite crystals are the ones we usually associate with snowflakes. The former, as the name suggests, is a plate-like, hexagonal crystal formed by coalescence with other crystals as it falls earthward. It can take shape in either moist or dry air, growing slowly when the air is moist, and much more rapidly in dry air.

The term "dendrite" means a figure resembling a tree, with its crystals so named because they once struck someone as looking like spreading branches. Actually, they resemble a star quite as much and so are also known as star or stellar crystals. The product of coalescence, they require moderately moist air for their formation. Six lacy, delicate arms, all looking like designs seen in a child's kaleidoscope, radiate out from their center.

Little needs to be said about snow and the ancients. In general, snow shared with frost a poor reputation — and for the same reasons: it was widely associated with the death of nature in

PLATE AND DENDRITE ICE CRYSTALS.

winter and the dangers of the season to human survival. But, because of its whiteness, it was also widely associated with the idea of purity. That whiteness was behind a later British peasant belief — that snowflakes were actually goose feathers. Out of this quaint outlook came an equally quaint Yorkshire rhyme:

> *Snaw, snaw, come faster,*
> *White as allybaster;*
> *Poor owd women pickin' geese,*
> *Sendin' the feathers down to Leeds.*

Much can be said about the place of snow in folk weathercasting. It has been the source of a wide assortment of predictions. We'll begin with one long-cherished in New England:

> *When the grouse drum at night, there will be*
> *a deep fall of snow.*

The proverb may have merit, on the grounds that perhaps the grouse, as are other animals in pre-storm weather, is made nervous by the conditions preceding a snow. Most snow forecasts, however, do not deal with its approach. Rather, the question at hand in most is how long a snowstorm can be expected to last. For example, there's this antique bit of reasoning:

> *When the first snowflakes are large, the snowstorm will be a lasting one. When they are small, the storm will be a short one.*

The forecast won't always work out for you, but it is based in meteorological fact. Large flakes result from strong atmospheric turbulence and heavy moisture. Both induce a multitude of midair collisions and excessive coalescence. Both the exaggerated turbulence and the heavy moisture promise a lasting storm.

> *If snow begins at mid of day,*
> *Expect a foot of it to lay.*

This one can't be trusted at all times either, but it shouldn't be totally ignored. Behind it is the fact that heavy storms often result when especially cold air moves in on late morning air that has had the chance to be well warmed.

> *When the snow falls dry, it means to lie.*
> *But flakes light and soft bring rain oft.*

The presence of the word "oft" indicates that whoever originated the forecast understood that it wouldn't apply every time. But, like the large-snowflake prediction, it, too, is based in meteorological fact. Dry snowflakes indicate that the atmosphere near ground level is moderately cold. Damp flakes hint that the temperature is rising and that it will melt the coming flakes and turn them into rain. Born of the same indications are:

> *Cut a snowball in half.*
> *Wet center means rain.*
> *Dry center can only be melted by the rain.*

> *When snow melts off the roof, the next storm will be rain. When the snow blows off, reckon on snow.*
>
> (An almost-to-the-word variation substitutes ice for snow.)

In addition to forecasts couched in proverbs, snow inspired a number of predictive beliefs, three of which now follow. They have a trait in common: all are without an ounce of validity. The last of the trio, however, might be amusing to try as an experiment, but should the results prove correct, please remember that you've run into nothing more than a happy coincidence. Born in Europe, it's a superstition that was long ago transplanted in the U.S. backwoods:

> *The date of the first snow foretells the number of snowstorms for the winter. Should the year's first snow, for example, come down on the twelfth of the month, you can expect twelve more storms before the winter's done.*

> *There will be as many snows in the winter as the moon is old at the time of the first snowstorm.*

> *Place on a stove a pint of snow from the season's first snowfall. When the snow begins to boil, count the number of bubbles rising to the surface. They will tell you the number of snowfalls due that winter.*

OTHER MOISTURES

We come now to three moistures familiar to us all — dew, frost, and fog. Are they not forms of precipitation, too, and thus entitled to be listed as members of the rain family? They certainly strike many people as being so. But this is an all-too-common misconception. Dew, frost, and fog do not shape themselves within the clouds and then fall to earth. Rather, they are the results of a distinct action that occurs at or near ground level. As such, they cannot be listed as types of precipitation.

DEW AND FROST

> *Frost or dew in the morning light*
> *Shows no rain before the night.*

Dew and frost must be considered together because, as the above prediction makes clear, they both forecast the same kind of weather.

Dew takes shape when water vapor in the air condenses and becomes visible. It is formed at night when the earth itself and all the objects at ground level radiate the heat gathered during the day and cool themselves to or below the condensation point of the atmospheric vapor around them. The vapor condenses, turns to water, and is seen as dew.

In brief, frost is simply frozen dew. It is born of the condensation that occurs when water vapor passes through atmosphere that is (or touches objects that are) below the freezing point. The vapor becomes visible as small ice crystals that, when thickly clustered, can easily be mistaken for snow. The vapor crystallizes immediately and does not pass first through a watery — or dewy — stage.

But is the above prediction true? No two ways about it, it is. Dew and frost in the morning unmistakably indicate the presence and continuation of clear weather. Both are most commonly formed on calm chilly nights in which the factors that presage rain — clouds, a backing wind, and a rising humidity — are absent. Dew by itself can be used to illustrate what is at work behind the forecast.

While the earth takes on heat from the sun during the daylight hours, it — and every object on it — surrenders that heat at night by radiating it back into the atmosphere. When any object (let's say a blade of grass in this instance) loses its heat, it simultaneously gains heat by the absorption of radiation from surrounding objects. On a clear, cold night, the temperature falls rapidly, causing the blade to surrender more heat than it is absorbing. Its temperature falls until it causes the air around it to condense and form dew.

But what of a pre-storm night? Clouds are present and reflect back some of the radiated heat. Added to the scene are that backing wind and rising humidity; both contribute a further warmth. Cooling is hampered and leaves everything from the blade of grass to the hood of your car free of dew.

The very same rules of nature are in play with frost — but on a particularly cold night.

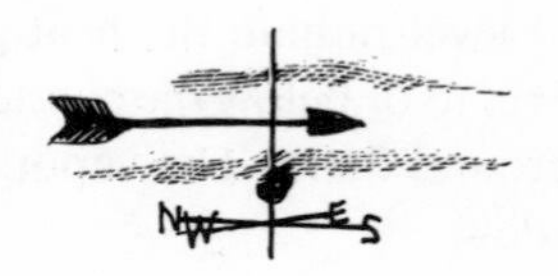

Dew: Prediction and Superstition

On its own, dew is responsible for two well-known prophecies. Each is quite different from the other, but both hold out the same promise:

> *When the dew is on the grass*
> *Rain will never come to pass.*

> *When you see cobwebs on the grass and in the fields*
> *at daybreak, you can be sure the day will be fair.*

— NEW ENGLAND

A word about those cobwebs. Almost impossible to see under ordinary circumstances, they do indeed indicate good weather when readily visible. They quickly catch the eye because they are coated with dew.

If dew announces the presence of good weather, then the absence of dew suggests quite the opposite. Present now are the unstable atmospheric conditions that make its formation impossible and promise a storm to come. Hence, we have:

> *When grass is dry at morning light,*
> *Look for rain before the night.*

> *When the morn is dry,*
> *The rain is nigh.*

And a combination of wet and dry in a masterpiece of terse British understatement:

> *Morn dry, rain nigh.*
> *Morn wet, no rain yet.*

A moisture that appeared for seemingly no reason on clear nights, dew was a mystery to the ancients. Coming with the dawn, that freshest part of the day, its purity was easily envisioned and it was soon thought to contain magical healing powers. This early belief was passed on to Europe, where dew was collected and used to improve the sight, put an end to goiter, and cure vertigo. In one English area, troubled parents turned to it as a means of restoring the physical strength of their sickly young.

For most of the ancients, however, dew was not simply revered for its healing powers. Along with all the natural phenomena we've mentioned thus far, it was regarded as something sacred. Some people believed that it came from the gods and variously thought of it as a divine blessing, a signal of divine protection, or a divine refreshment. Others held that it belonged to a god or was itself a deity. The North American Indians called it the spittle of their gods. Several European cultures looked on the dewdrop as the eye of a god. The early Christians often referred to Christ as the dew-man. The word "dew" itself is related to the French "dieu," meaning god.

Seen as it is at the break of a new day, dew early became associated with the ideas of youth and light. On the latter score, Oriental mythology contains a legend about the "tree of sweet dew." It was said to flourish on Kuen-Lun, a sacred mountain, and to send out its light from there to the world; the legend suggests that the light is not simply physical but spiritual and intellectual as well. Similarly, in other cultures, the legends that connect dew and light refer to intelligence, wisdom, inspiration, and spiritual illumination. In some early countries, it signified the doctor, the teacher, the sage, the priest.

On a less grand — but a far more charming — scale, dew is responsible for an English and Scottish superstition now several centuries old. Maidens who went out early on a May morning, collected the dew, and cleansed their faces with it were guaranteed great beauty for the remainder of the year. In parts of Scotland, they were also assured of good fortune for the year. For best results, the dew was to be gathered at the base of an oak tree.

Frost: Prediction and Superstition

> *Fine, clear weather usually follows heavy frosts.*

The prediction is a sound one. As was said earlier, all the rules of nature that are in play for dew are likewise in play with frost. The sky is clear and storm-free. The only difference here is that the atmospheric and ground temperatures are substantially lower.

> *Spider webs floating at autumn sunset,*
> *Bring a night frost, you may bet.*

Could be. A cold snap may well be at hand on an autumn night. And the fact that the web is "floating" indicates a still atmosphere that could produce frost or dew.

Unlike dew, frost did not enjoy a particularly happy reputation in the ancient world. Though in early Christendom it was associated with yuletide celebrations, it was widely regarded as signifying the death of nature that came with the winter season.

In mythology, frost was generally visualized as an elf, a wood sprite, or a wood nymph; in Russia, however, it was an old, white-haired man, Father Frost, and in Germany an aged and white-haired woman, Mother Frost. Regardless of its age or place of origin, the creature was always pictured as wearing a white robe sparkling with frost. One of these mythical beings remains with us today — Jack Frost. Said to be the visitor who traces the designs left on plants and windows touched by frost, Jack is thought to have originated in Scandinavia. Norse legend holds that he was the son of Kari, the god of the winds, and was named either Jokul or Frosti, with the former meaning "icicle" and the latter, of course, "frost." Over the centuries, the two were joined and, in English, were transformed into today's name for the imaginary fellow.

One of folklore's most entertaining predictions is this forecast based on the behavior of the American grasshopper, the katydid:

> *Listen to the katydid. When its chirp goes from "Katie-did" to "Katie," there will be frost in ten days.*

Perhaps the frost won't arrive in precisely 10 days, but the katydid's chirp is nevertheless widely trusted as a warning of an approaching cold snap. As with so many insects, a descending temperature numbs the katydid and temporarily reduces the strength and length of its call, taking it down through stages to "Katie" at 65°F., to "Kate" at 58°F., and then to total silence when the temperature goes below 55°F. By the time "Kate" is heard, you can pretty safely bet that a frosty or at least a chilly morning is in the making.

Now let's turn for a moment to another insect, the humble cricket. He can't predict a frost, but he is credited with being able to tell you when the temperature is low enough to make frost. In fact, weather lorists insist that the cricket can tell you the Fahrenheit temperature, whatever it may be. They so admire his accuracy that they long ago nicknamed him "the poor man's thermometer." To take advantage of his talents, all you need do is count his chirps for a time and then apply any of several rudimentary mathematical equations to the total.

One is to count the chirps for a minute, add 100 to their number, then divide the total by 4. Should you count 160 chirps, your equation will end up looking like this:

160 chirps plus 100 = 260
260 divided by 4 = 65°F.

Another method is to count the chirps for 15 seconds and then add 37. A variation states that the number of chirps in 14 seconds plus 40 is the formula to use. Louis D. Rubin, Sr., and Jim Duncan, in *The Weather Wizard's Cloud Book,* suggest that 32 be added to the number of chirps in those same 14 seconds.

But we have a problem here, regardless of how accurate the lorists insist the cricket is as a living thermometer. The two suggestions for 14-second counts don't match, with their totals always bound to miss each other by 8°. If the cricket chirps 30 times in those 14 seconds, here's what you end up with:

30 plus 40 = 70°F.
30 plus 32 = 62°F.

The separation is even wider between the 1-minute and 15-second computations. If, as given in the opening example, there are 160 chirps in a minute, the count for 15 seconds is 40. The resultant totals are 12° apart:

160 plus 100 = 260 divided by 4 = 65°F.
40 plus 37 = 77°F.

And so, what to make of all this? If the cricket is to be trusted, then some of the lorists have erred in their advice, and there is only one way to settle the matter: a thermometer, a cricket of your own, and your personal determination of who is right and who is wrong. (Personally, after an evening out in the back garden, I am tending toward the 14 seconds plus 37.)

If the cricket computations prove too frustrating, you might try the rhododendron as a natural thermometer. Its leaves, open at 60°F. and extending upward, fold steadily inward as the air about them cools. They are about a quarter of the way closed at 40°F., over halfway at 30°F., and fully closed at around 20°F.

FOG

Fog has often been described as a cloud that is touching the earth. The description is an accurate one. Both take shape when warmish air, on encountering cooler air, condenses and transforms itself into water droplets or ice crystals. The only real difference is that the cloud can be formed at any altitude, while the fog is always found lying at or very near ground level.

There are several types of fog, the most common of which are the radiation and advection fogs. Radiation fog — which is a somewhat fancy technical name for ground fog — occurs under the same conditions that produce dew. Needed is a clear, cool, and cloudless night that, first, enables the ground easily to radiate its daytime heat and then quickly lowers the temperature of the rising heat to the point of condensation.

Advection fog is generated when a mass of warmish, moist air moves in over a cooler mass. It is most often seen along seashores or above the surfaces of lakes and oceans.

Fog: Prediction and Superstition

Ancient beliefs about fog were, understandably, much the same as those that centered on the clouds and their mists. Its opaqueness, for example, was viewed by some cultures as a factor hiding the great truths of the universe from man; it was also thought by many to be a veil behind which the supreme deity concealed himself.

And it was, like the clouds, widely regarded as the breath of the gods. The Polynesians were among the peoples holding such a belief. In their mythology, the mists were the forlorn sighs of the earth goddess for the sky god after the two had been separated from each other by their child, the god of the forests.

In our own time, the fog has become synonymous with the idea of mystery and evil. We can credit the motion picture, with its offerings of horror and murder, for this most modern of "superstitions." What would a Sherlock Holmes or Frankenstein film be without its fog-shrouded castles, contorted trees, lonely moors, and British manors? And are not we moderns reacting to those special-effects mists just as the ancients reacted to the fog and the clouds? They seem to be mists that are hiding a truth from us — an unknown to be revealed at the film's end.

Fog has always played only a minor role in weather lore, prompting but a very few proverbs and superstitions down through the ages.

> *When Tottenham wood is all on fire,*
> *Then Tottenham street is nought but mire.*
>
> — ENGLAND

What this rhyme is saying is that, when the fog hangs over the woods like the smoke of a fire, you can count on a heavy rain to come. Locally, the forecast is on the mark. Just why it is can best be seen within the explanation of a much broader prediction:

> *A summer fog for fair,*
> *A winter fog for rain;*
> *A fact most everywhere,*
> *In valley and on plain.*

The radiation fog, coming of a clear and cloudless night, is most frequently seen from around midsummer to early autumn; thus, as does the presence of dew at daybreak, it suggests the continuation of fair weather. On the other hand, the advection fog is often seen in the winter when warmish, moist air moves in over very cold surfaces such as snow banks. The warm air may well be the advance guard of an atmosphere thick with rain-producing moisture. It is likely that the advection fog is often at fault for turning Tottenham street into "nought but mire."

> *Mists dispersing on the plains*
> *Scatter away the clouds and rain.*
> *But when they rise to the mountain top*
> *They'll soon descend in copious drops.*

This proverb is best explained by breaking it into two halves and looking at each half separately. Responsible for the opening two lines is an atmospheric condition that takes us back to a cloud prediction in Chapter Five:

> *When you see a cloud grow smaller and melt away, it is going to be fair.*

The cloud grows smaller because the sun's heat and the surrounding dry air are causing it to evaporate and fade away. The same thing happens to a radiation fog when the atmosphere a few hundred feet above the ground is comparatively dry. The sun's heat and the dry air, mixing itself with and overcoming the moist air, cause the fog to evaporate.

As for the proverb's closing lines, they, too, take us back to Chapter Five and another cloud proverb:

> *When the clouds are upon the hills,*
> *They'll soon come down by the mills.*

As warmish air moves up a mountainside, it steadily cools and eventually condenses into a cloud that can produce rain or snow near or at the mountaintop. That same upward movement may well create a fog that rises and mingles with the rain-producing cloud. Thus, though the cloud is principally responsible for the rain, the proverb credits the fog with descending in "copious drops."

New Englanders have expressed this in a couple of ways:

Fog on the hills,
More water for the mills.

When the fog goes up the mountain hoppin',
Then the rain comes down the mountain droppin'.

Now here, in its first line, is what appears to be a contradiction:

When the fog goes up, the rain is o'er.
When the fog comes down, 'twill rain some more.

Though seemingly a contradiction, the proverb's opening line is founded on a condition often seen near the end of mountain storms. Dry, cool winds arrive on the scene and disperse the clouds and fog, seeming to drive them up and away. As for the second line, a continuing rain-threatening moisture in the atmosphere will create more fog, more cloud, and a greater possibility of more rain.

Next, we return to the rain and its family members, beginning with the glorious rainbow. In common with so many other weather activities, they can produce phenomena ranging from the beautiful to the frightening. In the following two chapters, we're going to look at each extreme — one a beauty and the other a beast — and at the contributions each has made to the literature of weather lore.

CHAPTER EIGHT

The Beauty: The Rainbow

> *Triumphal arch, that fill'st the sky*
> *When storms prepare to part,*
> *I ask not proud Philosophy*
> *To teach me what thou art.*

— THOMAS CAMPBELL (1777–1844)
From: "To the Rainbow"

IT'S PRETTY SAFE to say that, in common with British poet Thomas Campbell, no one has ever gone unmoved on seeing the wondrous, multicolored span that cuts across the sky when the light of the sun mingles with falling rain. The rainbow has fascinated humans in every part of the world since the earliest of times, a fact clearly seen in the weather forecasting it has inspired, and even more clearly in the many ideas that took shape in antiquity to explain its presence and import.

THE RAINBOW AND THE ANCIENTS

With the similarity between the rainbow and a bridge being unmistakable, many ancient cultures were quick to see the resemblance and make it a part of their beliefs. Several North American Indian peoples, for instance, regarded it as a span between the physical and spiritual worlds, between heaven and earth. In the southeastern regions of the continent, the Catawba tribe believed it to be the road along which their dead walked to the hereafter. Far away in the Northwest, the Tlingit shared the same belief. A reverse view held sway in the Southwest, where the Pueblos said it was a bridge across which their earliest ancestors traveled to reach this world from what the tribesmen called "the worlds below."

The North American Indians were not alone in looking on the rainbow as a span between our world and another, as witness this old Scandinavian description:

| *The bridge to the gods.*

Along that bridge moved the souls of the dead to their final resting place. They made the journey safely if they had lived good, honorable, and courageous lives. Those unworthy of joining the gods were swept away by a great fire. The fire gave the rainbow its brilliant red band.

The early Japanese, while agreeing that the rainbow was a bridge, had a different concept of its purpose. Their mythology held that it was the span from which the gods Izanagi and Izanami cast the spear that created land.

Added to these views was the outlook that the ancient world held of all natural phenomena — that the rainbow was itself a deity or a belonging of a god. The Zulus of Africa thought it to be an evil spirit. A few cultures believed it was the serpent god that brought rain. To the Greeks, it was the spirit Iris, a messenger of the gods. One Siberian tribe thought it to be the hem of the sun god's coat. Another said it was his tongue. The early Jews and Christians likened the rainbow to Joseph's multicolored coat and called it a manifestation of God's love. Other groups, however, saw things differently. In such widely separated areas as India, Finland, and central Europe, it was the bow from which the lightning bolts of the thunder gods were shot.

The concept of the rainbow's arch as a bow is also found in early Jewish and Christian belief. In the wake of the Great Flood, Noah is said to have departed the ark, built a great fire, and offered up burnt sacrifices to God. In response, as reported in the

Bible, God promised not to inundate the world again and created the rainbow as a reminder of that promise:

> *I do set my bow in the cloud, and it shall be a token of a covenant between me and the earth. And it shall come to pass, when I bring a cloud over the earth, that the bow shall be seen in the cloud: and I will remember my covenant, which is between me and you and every living creature of all flesh: and the waters shall no more become a flood to destroy all flesh.*
>
> — GENESIS

Omens of Good and Evil

With their penchant for detecting signs of the future wherever they looked, the ancients could not pass up the opportunity of seeing the rainbow as a signal of coming good or evil. Today, perhaps because of its beauty, western cultures generally regard the rainbow as a sign of good luck, but for most ancients, it was both a happy and dreaded omen. To the Arawak Indians of South America and the Caribbean area, for instance, it promised good fortune when sighted above the sea. Above land, it loomed as an evil spirit in search of a victim.

The Iranian Moslems took their messages from its colors. A prominent red (the traditional color for anger and fire) meant war; yellow (associated with pestilence) promised death; and green (representing a compassionate and plentiful earth) foretold abundance.

The Roman author and naturalist Pliny the Elder (circa 23–79) was of a grim turn of mind so far as the rainbow was concerned. He claimed that it prophesied, at worst, a war or, at best, a miserable winter. A similarly pessimistic view — despite today's tendency to see the rainbow's appearance as fortunate — still prevails in parts of Europe and the United States:

| *It's bad luck to point at a rainbow.*

Why? Depending on local lore, either the sun or the storm god becomes angry on seeing a lowly human finger pointing in his direction. American Indians along the mid-Atlantic coast believed that the storm god departed in a huff and made the rainbow disappear. You and your pointing finger vanished along with it.

But the children of long-ago northern England had a method that was supposed to make the rainbow and its bad luck depart. They fashioned a cross of sticks on the ground and placed a small stone at the end of each stick. Straw was said to work as successfully as sticks.

Of Wealth Never Won

For reasons that have been lost in the mists of time but seem to be associated with man's desire to quest after something beyond his present state, the rainbow early became linked to the idea of great wealth. Throughout western culture, especially among the Irish, there lingers the old and altogether fanciful idea of the pot of gold to be had for the taking if only we can make our way across that splendid colorful arch to its very end. In the Silesian region of eastern Europe, an ancient myth has it that angels piled the gold there and that it can be claimed only by a nude man.

One end-of-the-rainbow superstition has nothing to do with wealth. In northeastern Europe, Romanian peasant lore holds that the ends of the rainbow stand in a river. Anyone who crawls to the river on hands and knees and then drinks the water from which the rainbow is rising will immediately change sex. A similar superstition is encountered in several areas elsewhere in Europe: anyone who passes beneath the rainbow's arch will likewise change sex. Why? Again, it's anybody's guess. Perhaps both ideas were born of humble and timid peasants as devices for keeping their ambitious and venturesome young from wandering off in search of a better life.

The pot-of-gold legend may have sprung from the human desire for something better in life, but there was also in the legend — and remains in it to this day — a suggestion of man's resignation to the likelihood that the quest will fail. The end of the rainbow can never be reached. With every hopeful step taken in its direction, that magnificent arch with all its promise recedes, stubbornly remaining just beyond reach because, like the mirage and so many human aspirations, it is an optical phenomenon.

WHY THE RAINBOW?

Today, the ancient religious and superstitious views of the rainbow are long gone in all but the most primitive regions of the world, replaced by the knowledge of what is actually happening when that breathtaking arch takes shape. We know that the rainbow is one of many optical phenomena that are created when the sun's white light passes through atmospheric areas of differing densities. The speed of the rays is altered, and they are refracted or bent as they pass from, say, warm air to cold air or, as in the case of the rainbow, from air to water. Under certain circumstances, the bending rays split themselves into the color bands of the spectrum — from red at one end to blue, indigo, and violet at the other.

In the rainbow, the results of this breakage become visible when you stand between the sun and a rain shower, with your back to the sun. The rays of sunlight penetrate each raindrop, with many then passing straight through. Others, however, strike the curving edges of the drop at the points where the surface makes an acute angle with the direction of the sunlight. Here, the drop not only bends the rays but, acting like a prism, splits them into their constituent colors. Bent and now wearing their colored garb, they

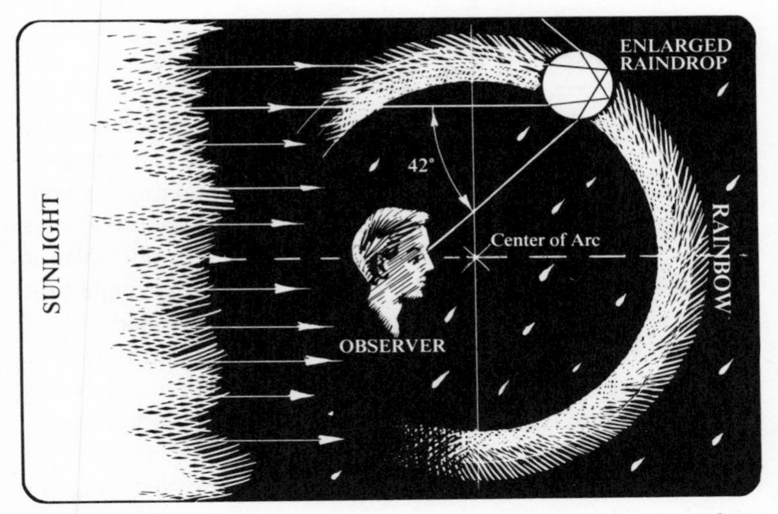

WHEN LIGHT STRIKES A RAINDROP, *many of its rays pass through it. However, along the curving edges, the drop acts like a prism and splits the rays into their constituent colors. The rays, wearing their colored garb, enter the drop, bounce off its inner surfaces, reflect themselves back out of the drop, and travel to the eye. The eye sees those colors as the rainbow.*

enter the drop, bounce off its inner surfaces, reflect themselves back out through the drop, and travel to your eye.

One, two, or several arches can be formed. The most visible of their number is colored red along its outer edge and violet along its inner edge, with shades of yellow, green, and blue between. Called the primary or common rainbow, it is made up of reflections from raindrops that are at an angle of about 42° from an imaginary line that runs from the sun, passes through your eye, and extends to a point on the ground ahead of you — a point that is directly below the center of the arch.

The rainbow is at its best and most spectacular when the sunlight is being reflected from large raindrops. The colors stand out brilliantly and are sharply differentiated. There is a loss of brilliance and color separation when the raindrops are small.

RAINBOW FACTS AND LORE

The pot of gold at rainbow's end can never be reached because the rainbow itself (with a rare exception or two) can never be reached. The arch recedes at our approach and remains, beckoning, in the distance. This is because its distance from us is always exactly that of the nearest and farthest raindrops responsible for its presence. Any step toward a rainbow adjusts our angle to it and the sun, causing the reflection to "move" farther back.

What are the exceptions? A rainbow can take shape above any watery surface, such as a pond, a waterfall, a fountain, or even a garden sprinkler. At times, you may sight a small rainbow hovering above a fountain or a sprinkler just a few feet away. If it's within arm's reach so that you need not step forward, you can extend your hand into its band.

Your angle to the sun and the distant arch is responsible for an especially interesting rainbow fact. When you stand alongside another person, both of you will see a rainbow but not the same one. Because of the difference in your individual angles, no matter how slight it may be, each of you will see your own "personal" rainbow.

As those fortunate pilots and airline travelers who have seen it will tell you, the rainbow can appear as a full circle on being sighted from the air. It shows itself as an arch when viewed at ground level because the curvature of the earth's surface hides the remainder of the circle.

If watched long enough, the arch will prove to be a varied thing, with its shape changing as the sun mounts higher and higher. When the sun is low to the horizon, the arch forms a semi-circle. But, as the sun ascends and changes the angle at which its rays strike the falling drops, it "flattens" the arch, an illusion caused by the fact that the arch is descending to the horizon. Once the sun is riding higher than 42° above the horizon, the rainbow cannot be seen. For this reason, the rainbow is most often on view in the early morning or in the mid to late afternoon and disappears sometime around noon. Should the rainbow be seen near noontime, the odds are that you are standing in a high northern latitude.

THE RAINBOW AS WEATHER PROPHET

In all parts of the world, the rainbow has long been respected as an adept rain prophet, as well it should be because, by its very nature, it is associated with wettish air. You'll find that the following predictions have a familiar ring to them. They are much the same as the red sky rain forecasts:

> *Rainbow in the morning,*
> *Shepherd take warning.*
> *Rainbow toward night,*
> *Shepherd's delight.*
> *Rainbow at noon,*
> *Rain very soon.*
>
> (The final two lines seem to contradict the point that the rainbow disappears sometime around noon. However, if the more general term, around midday, is substituted here, the two lines have merit.)

or

> *A rainbow in the morning*
> *Is the shepherd's warning.*
> *A rainbow at night*
> *Is the shepherd's delight.*
>
> (Both proverbs have also been long associated with the sea, with sailor being substituted for shepherd.)

Dog in the morning, sailor take warning.
Dog in the night, sailor's delight.

(Sailors of old called rainbows sun dogs.)

If there be a rainbow in the eve,
It will rain and leave;
But if there be a rainbow in the morrow,
It will neither lend nor borrow.

(The final two lines refer to the rare nighttime rainbow.)

A rainbow in the morn,
Put your hook in the corn.
A rainbow at eve,
Put your head in the sheave.

Rainbow in the eastern sky,
The morrow will be dry.
Rainbow in the west that gleams,
Rain falls in streams.

— CHINA

It is no accident that the rainbow forecasts resemble the red sky predictions. Much the same forces are at work in both types of forecast. The rainbow at sunset is being reflected off rain to our east while the sun is descending behind us in the west. (Remember, to see a rainbow, we must be looking at it while standing with our backs to the sun.) Hence, with the weather patterns in our latitudes being borne on westerly winds, the rain is being carried away from us and good weather is approaching. Conversely, the morning sun, rising in the east, is being reflected through wettish air to the west, with the result that rain is on the way.

Mariners have long wedded the rainbow and the wind in their predictions. For example:

Rainbow to windward,
Foul fare the day.
Rainbow to leeward,
Damp runs away.

(The second line often reads:
Foul fall the day.)

When the rainbow is in the wind's eye,
Rain is nigh.

The marriage is an apt one in our latitudes. A rainbow reflected from a windward sky signals that a rain cloud is being carried toward us. Reflected in the leeward sky, it indicates that the rain has passed to our east and is continuing on into the distance.

And there's yet another similar prediction based on the same reasons:

Rain is coming when a rainbow is seen in a cloud moving towards you. Rain is departing when a rainbow is seen in a cloud moving away from you.

The saying above speaks of the rainbow in somewhat pedestrian terms. A far more romantic vision of the earth and its beauty was expressed by British poet William Henry Davies (1871–1940) in his poem "The Rainbow." We close with his words:

Look, there's a rainbow now!
See how that lovely rainbow throws
Her jewelled arm around
This world, when the rain goes.

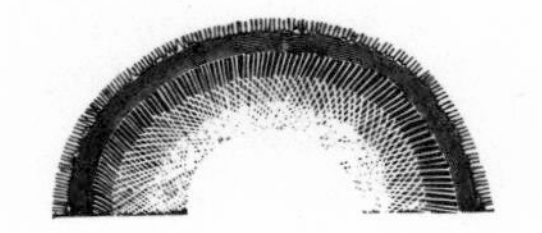

CHAPTER NINE

The Beasts: Thunder and Lightning

THESE BOISTEROUS companions — born an instant apart, sired by the same forces, but so different from each other — have triggered some of the most imaginative observations in the English language. There is, for instance, the reverent but straightforward comment by British statesman William Temple (1622–1699) that thunder is "the great artillery of God." As for lightning:

> *Life, struck sharp on death,*
> *Makes awful lightning.*

— ELIZABETH BARRETT BROWNING (1806–1861)
From: *Aurora Leigh*

> *The Lightning reached a fiery rod*
> *And on death's fearful forehead wrote*
> *The autograph of God.*

— JOAQUIN MILLER (1841–1913)
From: "With Love to You and Yours"

What is the world's delight?
Lightning that marks the night,
Brief even as bright.

— PERCY BYSSHE SHELLEY (1792–1822)
From: "Mutability"

And, in every part of the world, both have been the subjects of myriad folk beliefs. On a grand scale, many an ancient culture imagined thunder to be the speech of angry gods, and lightning to be the spears they sent hurtling through the sky. The Greeks were sure that thunderbolts were thrown by an outraged Zeus. For the Norse, the god of thunder was Thor, a red-bearded fellow whose awesome strength enabled him to forge thunderbolts. The Romans thought that the sound of thunder on the left heralded a message of special import from the gods.

On a lesser scale, there are the simple folk beliefs that took shape down through the centuries and remain with us to this day. Sometimes based on a reverential fear of what seemed to be supernatural occurrences and sometimes on personal but meaningless observations, they are beliefs that have all been shown to be empty of truth:

Lightning is attracted to mirrors.

Branches of the hazel tree, when gathered on Palm Sunday and then kept alive in water, will protect a house from thunder and lightning.

— ENGLAND

Lightning never strikes twice in the same place.

(This belief persists today despite much evidence to the contrary. It is reported that New York City's Empire State Building was struck sixty-eight times in a three-year period earlier in this century.)

Thunder curdles cream. Lightning sours milk.

(There may have been some truth to these two ideas in pre-refrigeration days, for milk and cream did show a tendency to act up during electrical storms. But it is suspected that such pre-storm atmospheric upheavals as rising humidity were the cause, rather than thunder and lightning.)

A thunderstorm in the winter means the death of an important man in the village or parish.

— WALES

Both thunder and lightning have inspired a number of folk predictions. Before we can comment on whatever meteorological truths may lie behind them, however, we need to know how the thunderstorm is born.

The trouble starts when warm, moist air just above ground level rises to mingle with a high-altitude layer of cold air. The meeting, causing the warm air to condense, fashions a giant cloud — the mountainous cumulonimbus — and creates within it violent updrafts that, when a genuinely fierce thunderstorm is in the making, can exceed speeds of 60 miles an hour. The updrafts drive the cloud, which is ballooning all the while because of the internal condensation, high into the sky. It is quite capable of ascending to 60,000 feet and has been known to attain heights of around 75,000 feet. At around the 60,000-foot mark, the cloud encounters the stable stratosphere. It then "flattens" along its top, spreads out (usually along a downwind tack), and takes on the look of a giant anvil, a look that is more than familiar to anyone who has ever lived in thunderstorm country.

The updrafts that mark the embryo stages of a thunderstorm are caused by any of three conditions. First, as commonly occurs in the American Midwest and East, they may be created by rising air that has been heated by radiation from the earth's surface. Second, as is often the case in Florida and other of the southeastern states, there may be sharp differences in the temperatures above the land and sea. Finally, the drafts may result when a cold front moves in during a warm or hot spell.

Of the three conditions, the arriving cold front brings the greatest trouble. When either of the first two conditions prevails, the resultant storm is — at least, by thunderstorm standards — on the tame side. It dazzles the eye with a few strokes of lightning, deafens with some thunder claps and their rolling echoes, and lets loose a heavy rain. But it usually lasts for just a few minutes or, at the most, somewhere between a half-hour and an hour, before moving off into the distance with its cloud. The cold front, however, produces the most severe and longest-lasting thunderstorms. They're apt to remain in the neighborhood for hours.

But back to the thundercloud itself. All is violent action within its growing mass — a mass that is white from the midriff up and an ominous gray-black at the base. The drafts whip its uppermost folds and it billows ever higher into the sky. It continues to balloon as condensation, collision, and coalescence form raindrops. Then, on meeting truly cold air, the water droplets come into contact with ice particles. Precipitation begins. On falling to lower levels, the raindrops and ice crystals cool the warmer air and cause downdrafts to take shape alongside the updrafts.

The raindrops and ice crystals are given a roller coaster ride through the atmosphere, a ride that can unleash a heavy rain and, not surprisingly, a hailstorm. The entire process climaxes when the first stroke of lightning spears down through the cloud and the first explosion of thunder is heard.

For some reason — perhaps because it is easier on the ear and tongue — we invariably refer to these phenomena as thunder and lightning. Actually, in the the chronology of their birth, they come in reverse order — first, lightning and then thunder.

WHEN LIGHTNING IS BORN

The exact cause of lightning remains something of a mystery to meteorologists, but in great part, it seems to be triggered by the colliding raindrops and ice crystals as they bounce about in the turbulent air. The friction of the incessant contacts creates a build-up of static electricity with its combination of positive and negative charges. For the most part, the lower regions of the cloud become negatively charged, and the upper areas positively charged. The charges collect steadily, developing a pressure that the atmosphere eventually finds intolerable. They explode in the awesome spark that is lightning. Sometimes, it is seen flashing behind the folds of the cloud and turning them white or yellowish-red for an instant. Sometimes, it flashes from cloud to cloud. And, sometimes, it spears out from the underbelly of the cloud and flickers between earth and sky. This latter course is less characteristic, for about 65% of all lightning flashes occur within or between clouds.

No matter whether seen within, between, or below the clouds, lightning always moves earthward. It does so because the lower regions of a thundercloud are mainly negatively charged and are thus attracted to the normally positively charged earth. The result of the attraction is a lightning stroke, which forms a path along which electricity can be conducted between the two. However, when we glimpse a lightning stroke, we are witnessing not just a single stroke but several.

There is, first, a downward stroke that, as it spears earthward, leaves a narrow channel of ionized air behind it. In the final split-second of its 60-mile-a-second journey, it is met with a stream of light from whatever earthbound object happens to be closest at hand. A complete electrical conducting path is instantly established, with the result that the earth gives off an awesome positive charge. Formed by that charge is a second stroke that sends an

LIGHTNING IS BORN *when a large positive charge takes shape in the upper areas of a cloud, while a large negative charge (in company with smaller positive charges) builds itself in the lower regions of the cloud. The negatively charged area is attracted to the customarily positively charged earth. In time, a lightning stroke cuts through the air to the earth. The earth answers with a positive discharge. It is this positive discharge that is seen as lightning.*

unbelievably powerful current — up to 30 million volts at 100,000 amperes — surging back along the narrow channel of ionized air to the cloud. The channel becomes so fiery hot that it glows with a heat of more than 54,000°F. It is the return stroke that we see as lightning.

What then follows is a series of three or more strokes from cloud to ground and from ground to cloud, all of them blending into a discharge lasting for a fraction of a second.

The fact that the down stroke is welcomed by the earthbound object closest at hand accounts for the traditional advice to stay well away from such tall objects as trees and church spires. The advice was long ago fashioned into this British rhyme:

> *Beware of an oak,*
> *It draws the stroke.*
> *Beware of an ash,*
> *It counts the flash.*
> *Creep under the thorn,*
> *It can save you from harm.*

If you're caught outdoors, the low-to-the-ground thorn figures to be a somewhat safer bet than the taller oak and ash — but, since it is outdoors, don't count on it. Today's safety rules advise you to take shelter in a low building or a car. Because lightning can set a building's roof afire, the car is advised as the better choice. Its metal body serves as a protective cage that sends the electrical charges streaming across its surface and into the ground via the tires. Just be sure not to touch the sides of the vehicle.

Old as it may be, the counsel to avoid trees is actually a johnny-come-lately to the weather lore scene. Throughout Europe and in parts of Asia, the people of earlier times thought that a wide variety of trees had the power to safeguard anyone who sheltered beneath them. For example, the oak was said to be sacred to the Norse god of thunder, Thor. The belief was that it not only provided a safe haven but afforded some extra protection as well. If its acorns and boughs were placed in a house, they protected the place from lightning.

The alder had a similar reputation. As the tree whose wood had gone into the Cross of Christ, it was considered sacred and was said to be safe from lightning strokes. It was also thought to protect nearby houses from being hit.

In Europe, a number of plants were likewise thought to be safeguards against lightning strokes. Christmas greens — especially the mistletoe that made its home in the admired oak — were supposed to safeguard a house for an entire year if placed in water and kept alive. A home was rendered immune not only from thunderstorms but also from fire when the roof was planted with houseleek or stonecrop. Anyone who carried leekwort was protected and given personal courage as well. Springwort had a special power. It drew the lightning and split the storm in half.

WHEN THUNDER IS BORN

Thunder is born in the instant when the return lightning stroke leaves the earth and spears upward through the channel of ionized air. The channel is viciously expanded outward and bursts in the sonic shock wave that reaches us as a thunder clap. That initial sound is followed by a rumble as the thunder echoes through the sky. The sound of the thunder always reaches us after we see the lightning flash because light rays travel at 186,282 miles a second while sound waves (whose speed varies with such factors as temperature) lope along at somewhere between 1,000 and 1,100 feet or so per second. This difference in speed enables us to tell just how far away the lightning is striking. All that needs be done is to count the seconds between the flash and the initial thunder clap. For every 5 seconds that elapse, the lightning is about 1 mile away.

PREDICTIONS AND PROVERBS

Thunderstorms move in so quickly and then depart with such haste that, unlike the rain, they have earned no predictions as to their arrival and length of stay. But there are a few predictions that refer to what will come in their wake, and at least one of these smacks of the truth:

> *When it thunders in the morning,*
> *It will rain before the night.*

This is more than a reasonable guess as to the immediate future. It is a well-established fact that the upward movement of warm, moist air responsible for the thunderstorm (and the rain that so often accompanies it) is usually more active in the afternoon than in the morning. Hence, if the atmospheric conditions permit a thunderstorm before noon, their increased activity in the afternoon can very likely bring rain.

Thunder predictions often concern themselves with what the storms may do to a farm crop. They are the inventions of those countless farmers who, down through the ages, have constantly observed the weather's various behaviors for some indication of the harm or benefit it promised at harvest time. For example:

> *Thunder in March betokeneth a fruitful year.*

> *When April blows her horn* [thunders],
> *It's good for both hay and corn.*

Both forecasts are based on the idea that thunderstorms in the early spring are customarily the result of a cold front moving in to choke off a period of unseasonable warmth. The warmth is usually on the mild side but is still dreaded because it threatens a dangerously early appearance of vegetation. The cold front promises to end the danger.

Not every farmer, however, agrees that an early-year thunderstorm is a boon, as witness:

> *When it thunders in March,*
> *It brings sorrow.*

> *March damp and warm,*
> *Does farmer much harm.*

The proverbs are built around a simple already-mentioned fact. When arriving early in the year, the atmospheric conditions responsible for thunderstorms can disrupt the orderly thawing process that produces healthy trees, vines, and grasses. Crops do best when the freezing ground of winter slowly thaws throughout the spring. The warmth that brings the early thunderstorm can cause the crops to begin a premature thaw, with the likelihood that a following cold snap will refreeze and damage them.

> *Thunder in February frightens the maple syrup*
> *back into the ground.*

At first glance, this New England proverb has a fanciful look to it because syrup comes not from the ground but from the sap of maple trees. Nevertheless, it is widely thought to have merit. The sap, like animals, may be sensitive to weather changes, with the pre-thunderstorm upheavals causing a decrease in its flow.

Now let's turn to lightning. Most lightning proverbs speak of what kind of weather can be expected in its wake. We'll begin with two, the second of which is one of weather lore's more imaginative jingles:

> *Red lightning foretells a dry spell.*

Yaller girl, yaller girl,
Flashing through the night,
Summer storms will pass you,
Unless the lightning's white.

The phrase "unless the lightning's white" is the key to an understanding of both proverbs. When white lightning presents itself, we are seeing it through clear air and are usually looking west. By itself, the clearness indicates a coming storm (remember how, in advance of rain, objects become sharper and appear to move closer) and the westerly position means that the storm is being blown in your direction. Red or yellow lightning is usually sighted in the distance and is being seen through dusty air (which provides the color). The presence of dry and dusty air between you and the strokes, while not actually indicating a "dry spell" as such, leaves no doubt that the thunderstorm is passing you by to one side or the other.

Lightning in the south
Brings little else but drought.

Drought is too severe a word here. The proverb is saying the same thing as the two that preceded it. With our weather coming on westerly winds, lightning in the south means that the storm is bypassing your area and leaving you untouched. The prediction would be quite as true were north or east to be substituted for south in the first line. An eastward sighting would mean that the conditions generating the thunderstorm have already passed out of your neighborhood.

Where lightning strikes,
Go build your well.

This one is worth a try if you're in need of a well. For a variety of complex reasons having to do with the speed with which they exchange electrical charges, lightning is attracted to water. Thus, trees with their roots embedded in an underground spring are often struck by lightning.

A THUNDERSTORM ODDITY

At times, the thunderstorm atmosphere gives off sparkling lights known as "brush" discharges. The most publicized of their number is St. Elmo's Fire, a reddish (when positively charged), bluish-green (when negatively charged), or white glow that flickers about trees, buildings, the wings of aircraft, the masts of ships, and even the heads of animals and humans. Though it has been known to blind pilots temporarily on striking their planes, it is a harmless phenomenon. It has been the inspiration for maritime superstitions dating back to ancient times.

St. Elmo's fire is actually named for St. Erasmus, the patron saint of Mediterranean sailors. His name was altered through the centuries, first to Sant' Ermo and then to St. Elmo. Often called St. Elmo's Light, this odd electrical discharge was attributed to various gods in pre-Christian times. It was thought by early Greeks and Romans to be a materialization of the twin gods, Castor and Pollux. Seafarers of the day believed that a double glow meant that their ship was under the protection of both gods and was thus safe from disaster; a single glow signaled bad luck for the voyagers. With the coming of Christianity, the Greeks attributed the glow to St. Helena, the empress who had once gone searching for the True Cross in the Holy Land.

The current name derives from the legend that St. Elmo, in the moments before losing his life in a storm at sea, promised his sailor friends that, whenever they faced shipwreck, he would return in some form to assure them that they would survive the ordeal. Soon thereafter, the lightning glow flashed on a masthead and was assumed to be a manifestation of the saint himself. In general since then, the appearance of the "fire" has meant good luck for seamen — as well it should for it usually appears only near the end of a storm.

But, the human imagination being what it is, the seamen could not leave well enough alone. In time, they gave the glow's behavior an assortment of meanings. If it lingered high up in the masts, it promised a fortunate voyage. But, if it rippled down to the lower rigging or the deck itself, bad luck lay over the horizon. And Lord help the man that it touched or hovered above in halo-like fashion. His death was close at hand, perhaps just beyond the next wave. Were a seaman to touch the light, his shipmates drew away, certain that he was toying with disaster.

* * *

As spectacular as it is and as frightening as it can be at times, the thunderstorm is nevertheless one of the most commonplace of weather upheavals. While most often seen in equatorial regions — some of which must put up with its visits for as many as 200 times a year — it is a global occurrence. Estimates hold that there are about 8 million lightning flashes worldwide each day. It is also estimated that, at the very moment you are reading these words, some 1,800 electrical storms are taking place in various parts of the globe.

CHAPTER TEN

Weather Lore the Year Round

ALONG WITH THE seaman, the farmer has stood a daily weather watch for centuries now. Together, they have looked for signs of weather changes due in the next hours or days, the farmer with an eye to what a rain or a dry spell could do to his land and crops, the seaman with the fear of what a high wind or a storm could do to his ship. Additionally, the farmer has always searched for clues as to what the weather held in store for him over a span of weeks and months to come.

Such long-range forecasting has been vital not only to his livelihood but to his very survival as well. He has spent his autumns looking for hints of the coming winter. Would it be severe or mild? Would it bring more snow than rain? Or more rain than snow? If he were able to answer such questions with any degree of accuracy, he could gain some idea of how best to treat his ground and the crops it would be wisest to plant. Would the winter, for instance, be most amenable to wheat? To corn? To hay? Or to potatoes?

In his need for such information, the farmer turns today to his country's weather services and their charts and forecasts. Also today, as in an earlier time, he looks to his almanacs, hoping that their prognosticators know what they are talking about, and might well swear by an almanac for a lifetime when the predictions in even one issue prove accurate. And, in an earlier time (as he continues to do to this day), he looked to the nature all about him — to the animals of the neighborhood, to the trees and plants, to the foods he grew and ate, and to the weather conditions in a season, a month, or a week.

Wherever he looked, he saw, or thought he saw, dozens of helpful indications, and he fashioned them into prophecies to guide both him and his neighbors. Sometimes, he was precisely or pretty much on the mark. Sometimes he reached questionable conclusions. And sometimes he was dead wrong, usually because some superstition (customarily born of a religious belief) clouded his vision or because he made the mistake of developing a "universal law" on a single happening or a collection of occurrences that were only coincidental.

In this chapter, we're going to look at his assorted long-range forecasts, beginning with those that speak, totally or in greatest part, the truth.

ON THE MARK

Long-range forecasting, even when attempted with today's weather equipment and computerized data, is always a chancy business. The weather simply refuses to be impressed by the scientific approach and continues to behave as it very well pleases, sometimes electing to be predictable, and just as often deciding otherwise. For yesteryear's farmer, it was a more than risky business. It is a testament to his eye and his wit that even some of his long-range forecasts were right on the mark at all — or even near it.

His best long-range forecasting came out of the winter months and was centered on the snows of the season and what they promised for his trees, vegetables, and winter grains when harvest time arrived. He knew that snow was one of nature's great boons for planted crops. It delayed the blossoming of fruit trees until a time when killing frosts were no longer probable. It protected seeds until well into the spring. And it prevented the alternate thawing and freezing that could damage wheat and other grains. What he always wanted was that long and consistently cold winter, the winter that would bring a gradual and healthy thaw.

What he feared most, as was pointed out when we were talking of Candlemas Day (February 2) in Chapter Two, were sudden warm spells during the first 3 months of the year. They induced premature thaws that, so experience showed, were more than likely to be followed by a refreezing that damaged or killed his developing crops.

Out of his knowledge of the good that a long and consistently cold winter could do came such optimistic truths as:

A snow year,
A rich year.

Year of snow,
Crops will grow.

Corn is as comfortable under the snow as an old
man under his fur coat.

— Russia

And a combination of optimism and pessimism:

Under water, famine;
Under snow, bread.

But what of the damage that a sudden burst of warmish weather and its premature thaw could do? That damage, which threatened economic disaster and starvation, inspired all the dire Candlemas Day proverbs that we saw in Chapter Two. In addition, it gave us these bleak sayings:

> *A green Yule makes a fat churchyard.*

> *January warm,*
> *The Lord have mercy.*

> *January wet,*
> *No wine you get.*

> *If you see grass in January,*
> *Lock your grain in your granary.*

> *Of all the months in the year,*
> *Curse a fair Februeer* [February].

> *A February spring is worth nothing.*

> *A wet March,*
> *A sad autumn.*

> *Summer in winter*
> *And a summer's flood*
> *Never boded England good.*

And, from Chapter Two, a repeat of what may be the three grimmest entries in weather lore, speaking as they do of the economic disaster that a warm February can bring to the farm and pasture:

> *A Welshman had rather see his dam* [wife]
> *on the bier,*
> *Than see a fair Februeer.*

On Candlemas Day, if the sun shines clear,
The shepherd had rather see his wife on the bier.

The shepherd would rather see the wolf enter his flock than see the sun on Candlemas Day.

But back to the optimistic side of things, first with this happy comment that applies to regions where snow is not a routine visitor:

After a rainy winter, a plentiful summer.

And with these observations of a winter turning gently and steadily into spring:

A peck of March dust and a shower in May
Makes the corn green and the fields gay.

A bushel of March dust is worth a king's ransom.

April showers bring May flowers.

TRUTH: PERHAPS, PERHAPS NOT

The farmer's long-range forecasts begin to run into trouble when we come to the conclusions he drew on looking at his animals, his crops, and the sky above. As so many of the proverbs in this book have already proven, the heavens and the life about him served well for short-range forecasting. But they were of little use when he attempted to look deeper into the future. Natural scientists have dismissed many of his conclusions on the grounds that he attributed what he saw to the weather when other factors were the causal agents. Other of his findings are considered to be, at best, debatable. Here now are some of the things he had to say, followed by the reactions of the natural scientists:

Animals

> *If you see that a chicken's or a turkey's feathers are very thick at Thanksgiving time, expect a hard winter.*

> *When the buffalo hide is thick, the winter will be cold.*
>
> — American Indian saying

> *A bad winter is betide*
> *If hair grows thick on the bear's hide.*
>
> — Ozark Mountains

The scientists hold that the farmer and other outdoorsmen made a mistake in forecasting a colder-than-usual winter on the basis of thicker-than-usual animal pelts and richer-than-usual bird plumage. They point out that especially healthy pelts and plumage are not induced by a sense of self-protection but are the results of a happy recent past. The rains of the spring provided an abundant food supply on which the creatures — and their coats or plumage — thrived. There is also the very practical view that pelts and plumage are thick not because the weather is about to be cold but because it is already cold.

But we come immediately to a coat prediction that has stopped the scientists cold. It is one of the most familiar animal forecasts in weather lore:

> *The amount of brown on the woolly bear caterpillar foretells the severity of the coming winter. The wider the band, the milder will the winter be.*

The brown band is found midway along the tiny animal's length, with black extending away to either side. Many farmers swear by the prediction and may be justified in their faith. Scientists have studied the woolly bear and have been bewildered to find that the prediction proves itself out more times than not. No one can say whether the size of the band and the severity of the winter add up to coincidence or whether the little creature is actually blessed with some sort of internal "weather crystal ball."

And now a cherished but much doubted adage:

> *When squirrels lay in a large store of nuts, the winter will be a hard one.*

The squirrel, so the scientists say, works especially hard at his collecting not because he senses a coming time of want but because nature, in a given year, has chosen to provide him with a particularly rich food supply. If the year nets him a slender crop, then that is what he must contend with, no matter how severe or mild the winter eventually proves to be.

But, scientists say what they will, you may have a difficult time getting anyone who believes in the adage to agree with them. A friend who lives in California's Sierra foothills says that she has seen years when the squirrels around her place appear "almost frantic" as they dash about building their winter storehouses, and other years when, after a time, they casually ignore piles of nuts still left lying about. She insists that the "frantic" seasons have always been followed by severe winters, while the "casual" seasons have ushered in mild winters.

The scientists also dismiss the following as false, saying that the condition of an animal's bones has as little to do with the coming weather as do pelts and plumage:

> *When the Thanksgiving turkey's breastbone is dark, it indicates a hard winter to come.*

> *If the Thanksgiving chicken's breastbone is light, there will be much snow that winter. If dark, there will be little snow.*

Plantings

> *Onion skins very thin,*
> *Mild winter coming in.*
> *Onion skins very tough,*
> *Winter's going to be very rough.*

— MIDWEST

> *Look for a heavy winter when the buds have heavy coats.*

— MAINE

> *If corn husks are thicker than usual, a cold winter is ahead.*

— MIDWEST

> *When the corn wears a heavy coat, so must you.*

— PENNSYLVANIA

> *A tough apple skin means a hard winter.*
>
> (In New England, the proverb specifies tough apple skins in the autumn.)

There is a division of opinion among scientists here. Some contend that plants are no more able to foretell the temper of a coming season than are animals. On the other hand, there is more than a suspicion that the proverbs have merit. Heavy bud coats, corn husks, and apple skins do show themselves in advance of an extremely cold winter. It is thought that two basic weather facts are in play here. First, a warm, wet summer encourages plant growth; second, the weather averages out certain of its conditions by swinging like a pendulum. Put the two facts together and it becomes a possibility that a pendulum swing is going to bring a cold, dry winter in the wake of a warm, wet summer.

There is, however, one proverb in this category that is accepted as reliable:

> *Oak before ash, all wet and splash.*
> *Ash before oak, all fire and smoke.*

The rhyme is an old English one, with "fire and smoke" meaning drought. Its reliability stems from the fact that good crop growth fits in more closely with the annual emergence of the oak tree than with that of the ash, because the oak is known to bud before the ash in a normal growing season. The ash, however, usually buds before the oak when the soil is drier than usual. Thus, an early budding ash indicates a time of dryness, or drought.

There are several variations of the proverb, among them this pragmatic jewel:

> *If the oak's before the ash,*
> *The farmer's pockets are full of cash.*
> *If the ash is before the oak,*
> *The farmer's hopes will end in smoke.*

The Sky

When the farmer looked at the sky and used what he saw there to foretell the weather in the next hours or days, he was often right. Not so, however, when the sky became the source of long-range forecasting. The problem was that he tried to predict specific patterns and repeating behaviors on the basis of a presently seen weather condition. The weather, of course, repeats itself throughout the course of the years, but customarily only in such general terms as bringing warmth in the summer and cold in the winter. It is the product of too many conflicting and changing forces ever to repeat itself consistently in the specific terms that the farmer had in mind. Thus, if the following proverbs and beliefs ever do work out, the credit must go to coincidence:

> *The number of fogs in autumn tells the number of snows in winter.*

> *The date of the month on which the first snow falls gives the number of storms that the winter will bring.*

> *Full moon in October without a frost,*
> *No frost till full moon in November.*

> *So many mists in March,*
> *So many frosts in May.*

Days and Dates

> *The weather on the last Friday of the month tells you the weather for the next month. If the day is windy, the next month will be windy. If the day is fair, the next month will be fair.*

> *If Janiveer's* [January's] *calends by summerly gay,*
> *'Twill be winterly weather till the calends of May.*
>
> ("Calends" means the first day of the month.)

> *The direction of the wind on Ash Wednesday will remain throughout Lent.*

Here, again, there is no argument whatsoever that the farmer — along with all the others who attempted the same kind of forecasting — was miles off the track. The problem is identical to that of the sky forecasts. He was attempting to predict specific patterns and repetitions in behavior on the basis of the conditions on a given day. It was a futile enterprise that could succeed only with the help of coincidence.

Many of the early farmer's predictions were centered on religious feast days. On several counts, they have been dismissed as false. For one, they are based on the empty premise that the weather on one day will produce patterns and repeated behaviors in the future. For another, there is the argument that the farmer was reading a special weather import into a day because it happened to have religious significance:

> *A pleasant Easter Sunday means a bountiful harvest.*

The leap in imagination that brought the proverb into being seems almost too obvious to mention. For the early Christian, Easter, as a day of resurrection and rebirth, symbolized two of his deepest yearnings — his desire for immortality and his hope of starting life anew after each of his stumbles, each of his errors. How easy it was to think that happy weather on that day promised a future wonder for his survival and that of his loved ones.

Further, some of the forecasts have been criticized for reflecting a belief in miracles and in biblical writings rather than an understanding and acceptance of weather realities. For a case in point here, we can refer back to Chapter Six and the St. Swithin's predictions, which called for rain on that day to be followed by a Biblical 40 days' worth of downpours.

Finally, there is the fact that most of the religious feast days were established according to the calendar developed under Julius Caesar in 46 B.C. His Julian calendar remained in use until the 16th century when it had fallen 10 days out of cadence with the seasons. It was replaced by the Gregorian calendar, which, to straighten things out, immediately dropped 10 days from the year 1582. The deletion caused a shift in the days on which the feasts fell. Yet no one seemed bothered by the fact that the feast-day proverbs themselves were not changed a whit.

But, despite these assorted arguments, many of the feast-day predictions cannot be dismissed out of hand. This is because they apply to specific-day predictions that have merit when applied to the time of the year in which the day falls. The Candlemas Day forecasts, for instance, though restricting themselves to the appearance of warm weather on February 2, gain credence when we think of them as speaking of the damage that developing crops can suffer when hit by a sudden warm spell during the opening 3 months of the year.

Whether totally false or imbued with some germ of truth, the feast-day predictions make fascinating reading, as seen in the collection that follows. Many of the predictions, incidentally, will seem to contradict each other. Contradiction does play a part, but not so much as do four other factors: local weathers (which can so differ from one another), times of the month, religious hopes for what the weather of a feast day portended, and local interpretations of what was intended by certain wordings. The often-heard phrase "bright and clear" could mean a clear and cloudless cold day in one locality, but a clear, warm day in another.

JANUARY

March in Janiveer,
Janiveer in March, I fear.

Remember on St. Vincent's Day,
If the sun his beams display,
Be sure to mark the transient beam,
Which through the casement sheds a gleam;
For 'tis a token bright and clear
Of prosperous weather all the year.
(St. Vincent's Day is January 22.)

If St. Paul be fair and clear,
It promises then a happy year;
But if it chance to snow or rain,
There will be dear all sorts of grain;
Or if the winds do blow aloft,
Great stirs will vex the world full oft;
And if dark clouds do muff the sky,
Then fowl and cattle oft will die.
(January 25)

FEBRUARY

One would rather see a wolf in February
Than a peasant in shirt sleeves.

— GERMANY

If in February there be no rain,
'Tis neither good for hay nor grain.

If there is snow on St. Bridget's Day, the ditches will be filled with rain come spring.

(February 1)

When the wind is in the east on Candlemas Day,
There it will stick till the second of May.

(February 2)

Half the wood and half the hay
You should have on Candlemas Day.

This last entry, of course, is not a prediction, but the farmer's understanding that his winter stores should be about half used by early February. He would survey his stocks at this time and, on finding them more than half depleted, would make sure that he immediately added to them. In many areas, it was his custom to visit his neighbors to see and discuss the amounts of their remaining supplies. Were his stocks low and a friend's plentiful, there would likely be some bargaining right on the spot. He often did the same thing at Christmas.

If the sun doth smile on St. Eulalie's Day,
Good for apples and cider, they say.

(February 12)

The weather on the night of St. Peter's Day foretells the weather for the next forty days.

(February 22)

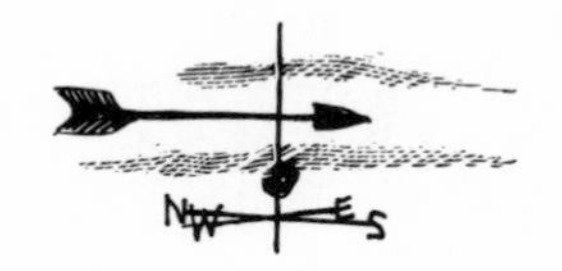

MARCH

When March comes in like a lion, it goes out like a lamb. When it comes in like a lamb, it goes out like a lion.

St. Winwaloe comes as if he were mad.

(Meaning a very windy day.)
(March 3)

St. Joseph's Day clear,
So follows a fertile year.

(March 19)

Rain on St. Benoit's Day means rain for forty days.

(March 21)

A clear St. Mary's Day [The Annunciation],
A fruitful year ahead.

(March 25)

The March sun causes dust,
And the winds do blow it about.

The March sun raises,
But dissolves not.

(Meaning that the sun does not give sufficient heat to melt any lingering snow or frost.)

APRIL

A soft dropping April brings milk to cows and sheep.

— IRELAND

A cold April the barn will fill.

Better April showers than the breadth of the ocean in gold.

— Ireland

If St. Vincent's Day is fair, there will be more water than wine.

(April 5)

Rain on St. Mark's Day betides ill for fruit crops.

(April 25)

MAY

Dry May,
Wet June.

Cold, wet May,
Barn full of hay.

A cold May and a windy
Makes a barn full and findy.

("Findy" means plentiful or substantial.)

A May flood never did anyone good.

Cold weather always falls on May 11, 12, and 13.

St. Pancras Day never passes without frost.

(May 12)

JUNE

Wet June,
Dry September.

If on the eighth of June it rain,
It foretells a wet harvest, men sain.

When rain falls on St. Barnabas Day, it is good for grapes.

(June 11)

If St. Vitus Day be rainy weather,
It will rain for thirty days together.

(June 15)

JULY

No tempest, good July,
Lest corn look ruely.

If the first of July it be rainy weather,
'Twill rain more or less for four weeks together.

Rain on St. Mary's Day means rains for a month.

(July 2)

If there is rain on St. Martin Bullion's Day, there will be rain for forty days.

(July 4)

> *If it rains on St. Anne's Day, it will rain for a month and a week.*
>
> (July 26)

Or, to repeat a prediction in Chapter Six:

> *If it rains on July 26, it will rain for the next two weeks. If the day is dry, you may expect two weeks of dry.*

AUGUST

> *Fair weather on St. Lawrence's Day presages a fair autumn.*
>
> (August 10)

SEPTEMBER

> *Matthew's Day bright and clear*
> *Brings good wine in next year.*
>
> (September 2)

> *As many floods will follow as the moon is old on St. Michael's Day.*
>
> (September 29)

OCTOBER

> *October has twenty-one fair days.*

No rain on St. Gallus Day, a dry spring will come.
(October 16)

St. Simon's is never dry.
(October 28)

NOVEMBER

If the beech acorn is wet on All Saint's Day,
the winter will be wet.
(November 1)

Where the wind is on Martinmas Eve,
There it will be for the rest of winter.
(November 10)

If the weather is dry and cold on St. Martin's Day,
the winter will not last long.
(November 11)

DECEMBER

The weather on Christmas foretells the weather
for the coming year.

Green Christmas,
White Easter.

If windy on Christmas,
Trees will bring much fruit.

Predictions and comments by the dozen have taken us, month by month, through the course of a year. But one more stroll through the year is in order, this time in the witty company of England's Irish-born politician and dramatist, Richard Sheridan (1751–1816). The journey, capturing the principal mood of each month, takes a mere twenty-four words:

SHERIDAN'S RHYMING CALENDAR

January snowy,
February flowy,
March blowy,
April showery,
May flowery,
June bowery,
July moppy,
August croppy,
September poppy,
October breezy,
November wheezy,
December freezy.

Without Comment: A Collection of Folk Predictions, Proverbs, Beliefs, Wisdoms, and Fancies

In this book we've dealt with several hundred predictions and beliefs, attempting to explain why some are true, some partly true, and some total fancy. But so many more remain. They are listed in this section, all without comment as to their validity (but with a note now and again to explain the intent of a vaguely worded proverb or to define certain of the terms within it). Perhaps, on the basis of what you have read thus far, you'll be able to decide which have validity to them — and to what degree.

ANIMALS

On the first of March,
The crows begin to search;
By the first of April,
They're sitting still;
By the first of May,
They've all flown away,
Coming greedy back again,
With October's wind and rain.

— England

Seagull, seagull, get thi [sic] *on t' sand,*
It'll never be fine while thou'rt on t'land.

(Based on sea gulls observed flying inland at the approach of stormy weather.)

— ENGLAND

If the cock moult before the hen,
We shall have weather thick and thin;
But if the hen moult before the cock,
We shall have weather hard as a rock.

If you rub a cat's back the wrong way and see sparks, cold weather is in the making.

The Cat [sic] *on your hearthstone to the day*
presages,
By solemnly sneezing, the coming of rain.

— ARTHUR GUITERMAN (1871–1943)
From: "The First Cat"

When a cat washes her face over her ear,
'Tis a sign the weather will be fine and clear.

When the glow-worm lights her lamp,
The air is always damp.

When frogs are jumping about more than ever, expect rain. But when they are piping in the evening, the next day will be fair.

When pigs carry sticks,
The clouds will play tricks.
When they lie in the mud,
No fears of a flood.

("Sticks" mean straw in the pig's mouth.)

It is a sign of good weather when fireflies are seen in great number.

You can expect rain when:

Bats fly into the house or make a great deal of noise.

Bears are restless.

The bull leads the herd to pasture.

Cattle lie down on going out to pasture.
(In many regions, New England among them, it is said that the cattle lie down because they feel rheumatic due to the changing air pressure.)

Cats wash behind their ears.

Cows don't give milk.

Crickets are chirping in the house.

Deer and elk come down from the mountain.
(In some areas, they are said to do so at least 2 days before a storm.)

Dogs' tails straighten.

Goats bawl, leave the high ground, and seek shelter.

Horses pull back their lips and grin.

Ladybugs swarm.

Mules shake their harnesses.

Owls hoot.

Sheep leap and frisk about.

Spiders abandon their webs.

Spiders spin webs in the grass during Indian summer.

CLOUDS

Clouds moving in opposite directions mean rain in about twelve hours.

(In some areas, the prediction is for rain in 2 hours.)

When the moon is old, a cloudy morning promises a fair afternoon.

Cloudy mornings turn to clear afternoons.

Cold is the night,
When the stars shine bright.

DEW

When the morn is dry,
The rain is nigh.
When the morn is wet,
No rain you get.

The dews of evening industriously shun,
They're the tears of the sky for the loss of the sun.

— Earl of Chesterfield (1694–1773)

EARTH AND WATER

Whitecaps on a pond or a river mean that it is going to rain.

When apple blossoms bloom at night,
For fifteen days no rain in sight.

When the chickweed blossoms are open, don't expect rain for at least three hours.

Holly berries shining red,
Mean a long winter, 'tis said.

— ENGLAND

We knew it would rain, for the poplars showed
The whites of their leaves.

— THOMAS BAILEY ALDRICH (1836–1907)
From: "Before the Rain"

FOG

The number of fogs in autumn tells the number of snows in winter.

When the mist comes from the hill,
Then good weather it doth spill;
When the mist comes from the sea,
Then good weather it will be.

Fog in the morning,
Sailor take warning.
Fog at night,
Sailor's delight.

So many mists in March,
So many frosts in May.

For every fog in March,
There'll be a frost in May.
A northern harr brings
Fine weather from afar.
("Harr" means mist.)

Three foggy mornings and then comes rain.

Three foggy mornings will bring rain three times harder than usual.

— NEW JERSEY

A misty winter brings a pleasant spring;
A pleasant winter a misty spring.

— IRELAND

Fog from seaward, weather fair;
Fog from land brings rainy air.

— MASSACHUSETTS

FROST

Many frosts and many thowes
Make many rotten yowes.
("Thowes" are thaws. "Yowes" are ewes.)

There will be frost just three months after the first katydid is heard.

— KENTUCKY

The frost is out of the ground when you hear the first frogs in spring.

A white frost never lasts more than three days.

Three white frosts and next a storm.

Heavy frosts are generally followed by fine clear weather.

The first and last frosts are the worst.

Frost and fraud both have always foul ends.

He that is surprised with the first frost feels it all winter after.

Black frost lasts longer than white frost.

(White frost is ordinary frost. Black frost is ordinary frost covered over with glaze. The glaze renders the frost transparent and enables one to see the ground beneath it. The visible earth tones darken the frost. Hence, the name "black frost.")

HOME

If you blow out a candle and the wick smolders for a longer time than usual, expect rain. If the wick goes out quickly, look for fair weather.

When camphor "riles" in its bottle, rain is coming.

MOON

In the old of the moon,
A cloudy morning bodes a fair afternoon.

When snow comes with the new moon, it will melt quickly. If the moon is old, the snow will likely last.

It never storms when the moon is nearly full.

— Kansas

When the moon is low in the south during February, it means thirty days of good weather.

Moon in the far north, expect cold weather.
Moon in the far south, expect warm weather.

Two full moons in a calendar month will bring heavy rain or a flood.

RAIN

Small showers last long,
But sudden storms are short.

— Shakespeare
From: *Richard III*

Some rain, some rest.
More rain, more rest.
(An invention of tired farm workers.)

— ENGLAND

or

More rain, more rest,
More water will suit the ducks best.

If it rains before church on Sunday, it will rain all week long.

When the sun shines during a rain, there will be rain tomorrow.

Sunshine and shower,
Rain again tomorrow.

If the rain comes before the wind,
Lower your topsails and take them in;
If the wind comes before the rain,
Lower your topsails, and raise them again.

Rain from the east,
Wet two days at least.

Rain comes scouth
When the wind's in the south.
("Scouth" means heavily.)

Small rain lays great dust.

Rain always comes out of Mobberley hole.

(The direction from which rain or a harsh wind comes was known to English peasants as a "hole.")

It rains by the planets.

(Dates back to the early astrological belief that the positions of the planets determined the weather.)

When England wrings,
Thanet sings.

(The Isle of Thanet on the coast of Kent requires much rain because of its dry, chalky soil.)

A Kerry shower is for twenty-four hours.

— IRELAND

Pity the man drowned in the storm, for after the rain comes the sunshine.

— IRELAND

RAINBOWS

Two rainbows at a time promise rain.

SEASONS

A good year is always welcome.

One swallow never made a summer.

— IRELAND

Autumn days come quickly like the running of a hound on the moor.

— IRELAND

SNOW

The north wind doth blow
And we shall have snow.

Snow for a se'nnight is a mother to the earth, for ever after a stepmother.

("Se'nnight" means a week.)

SUN

When the sun sets in a bank,
A westerly wind you will not want.

Where the sun enters, the doctor does not.

or

When the sun rises, the disease will abate.

The sun does not shine on both sides of the hedge at once.

(The meaning here can be interpreted as being the same as that in "You can't have your cake and eat it, too.")

The sun is never the worse for shining on a dunghill.

THUNDER AND LIGHTNING

Winter thunder bodes summer hunger.

Winter's thunder and summer's flood do not bode good for Englishmen.

Dunder do gally the beans.

— ENGLAND

("Gally" means frighten. The proverb is saying that thunder hastens bean growth.)

WEATHER

The mountains make their own weather.

Some [people] *are weatherwise,*
Some are otherwise.

— BENJAMIN FRANKLIN

For the man sound in body and serene in mind, there is no such thing as bad weather; every sky has its beauty, and storms which whip the blood do but make it pulse more vigorously.

— GEORGE GISSING (1857–1903)
From: *The Private Papers of Henry Ryecroft*

Cold weather and knaves
Come out of the north.

Cold weather is coming when the fire snaps and sparkles.

As the day lengthens,
The cold strengthens.

Windfrost is a good steward.

(Meaning there is less need for supervisors to watch their workers when the weather is cold; the men work harder to keep warm.)

When you take a teakettle from the stove and see sparks on the bottom, it is a sign of cold weather.

WIND

A northwest breeze as big as a sheet,
And the sails'll take no harm tonight.

North and south, the sign of drought.
East and west, the sign of blast.

A southerly wind and a cloudy sky proclaim a hunting morning.

A southerly wind with showers and rain
Will bring the wind from the west again.

No weather is ill
If the wind be still.

When the wind goes opposite the sun,
Trust it not, for back it'll come.

When the wind veers against the sun,
Trust it not, for back 'twill run.

As the wind blows, you must set your sails.

If the wind follows the sun's course, expect fair weather.

It is a bad wind that doesn't blow for someone.

— IRELAND

In his shepherd's calling he was prompt,
And watchful more than ordinary men.
Hence had he learned the meaning of all winds,
Of blasts of every tone; and oftentimes,
When others heeded not, he heard the South
Make subterraneous music, like the noise
Of bagpipes upon distant Highland hills.

— SIR HUMPHREY DAVY

A Final Sigh of Resignation

In recognition of the weather's successful insistence on doing as it pleases, when it pleases, and where it pleases:

Whether the weather be fine,
Whether the weather be not;
Whether the weather,
Whatever the weather,
Whether we like it or not.

— BRITISH SCHOOL RHYME

Recommended Reading

Battan, L. J., *Weather in Your Life.* New York: W. H. Freeman, 1983.

Bombaugh, C. C., *Harvest Fields of Literature: A Mélange of Excerpta.* Cincinnati and St. Louis: A. D. Worthington and Nettleton, 1895.

Cantzlaar, G. L., *Your Guide to the Weather.* New York: Barnes and Noble, 1964.

Cirlot, J. E. (Translated from the Spanish by Jack Sage), *A Dictionary of Symbols.* New York: Philosophical Library, 1962.

Emrich, D., *Folklore on the American Land.* Boston: Little, Brown, 1972.

Evans, I. H., Editor, *Brewer's Dictionary of Phrase and Fable.* New York: Harper & Row, 1981.

Fergusson, R., *The Penguin Dictionary of Proverbs.* Harmondsworth, Middlesex: Penguin Books, 1983.

Forrester, F., *1001 Questions Answered about the Weather.* New York: Dodd, Mead, 1957.

Gaffney, S., and Cashman, S., Editors, *Proverbs and Sayings of Ireland.* Portmarnock, County Dublin: Wolfhound Press, 1974.

Gilliam, H., *Weather of the San Francisco Bay Region.* Berkeley: University of California Press, 1962.

Greenler, R., *Rainbows, Halos, and Glories.* London: Cambridge University Press, 1980.

Hardy, R., Wright, P., Kington, J., and Gribbin, J., *The Weather Book.* Boston: Little, Brown, 1982.

Harrowven, J., *The Origins of Rhymes, Songs, and Sayings.* London: Kaye and Ward, 1977.

Hazen, W. B. and Dunwoody, H. H. C., *Signal Service Notes No. IX: Weather Proverbs.* Washington, D.C.: Government Printing Office, 1883.

Heuer, K., *Thunder, Singing Sands and Other Wonders.* New York: Dodd, Mead, 1981.

Humphreys, W. J., *Weather Proverbs and Paradoxes.* Baltimore: Williams & Wilkins, 1923.

Johnson, C., *What They Say in New England.* New York: Columbia University Press, 1963.

Jones, G., *Dictionary of Mythology Folklore and Symbols.* New York: Scarecrow Press, 1962.

Kohn, I., *Meteorology for All.* New York: Barnes and Noble, 1946.

Leach, M., Editor, *Funk and Wagnall's Standard Dictionary of Folklore Mythology and Legend.* New York: Funk and Wagnall's, 1950.

Lee, A. , *Weather Wisdom.* Garden City: Doubleday, 1977.

Lehr, P. E., Burnett, R. W., and Zim, H. S., *Weather.* New York: Golden Press, 1975.

Ludlum, D., *The Country Journal New England Weather Book.* Boston: Houghton Mifflin, 1976.

Radford, E. and M. A. (Edited and revised by Christina Hole), *Encyclopedia of Superstitions.* London: Hutchinson of London, 1961.

Riehl, H., *Introduction to the Atmosphere, 3rd Edition.* New York: McGraw-Hill, 1978.

Rubin, Sr., L. D., and Duncan, J., *The Weather Wizard's Cloud Book.* Chapel Hill: Algonquin Books of Chapel Hill, 1970.

Salanave, L. E., *Lightning and Its Spectrum.* Tucson: University of Arizona Press, 1980.

Smith, W. G., *The Oxford Dictionary of English Proverbs.* London: Oxford University Press, 1970.

Tallman, M., *Dictionary of American Folklore.* New York: Philosophical Library, 1959.

Taylor, A., and Whiting, B. J., *A Dictionary of American Proverbs and Proverbial Phrases, 1820–1880.* Cambridge: Belknap Press of Harvard University Press, 1958.

Trewartha, G. T., and Horn, L. H., *An Introduction to Climate, 5th Edition.* New York: McGraw-Hill, 1980.

Walsh, W. S., *Curiosities of Popular Customs and of Rites, Ceremonies, Observations, and Miscellaneous Antiquities.* Philadelphia: J. B. Lippincott, 1898; Detroit: Gale Research, 1966.

Index